WONDER-UNDER®

book of

EASY APPLIQUÉ

Oxmoor
House®

Wonder-Under® Book of Easy Appliqué
from the *Fun with Fabric* series

©1997 by Oxmoor House, Inc.
Book Division of Southern Progress Corporation
P.O. Box 2463, Birmingham, Alabama 35201

Published by Oxmoor House, Inc.,
and Leisure Arts, Inc.

Library of Congress Catalog Card
    Number: 97-66728
Hardcover ISBN: 0-8487-1571-3
Softcover ISBN: 0-8487-1572-1
Manufactured in the United States of America
First Printing 1997

Editor-in-Chief: Nancy Fitzpatrick Wyatt
Senior Crafts Editor: Susan Ramey Cleveland
Senior Editor, Editorial Services: Olivia Kindig Wells
Art Director: James Boone

Wonder-Under® Book of Easy Appliqué
Editor: Catherine Corbett Fowler
Contributing Editor: Patricia Wilens
Editorial Assistant: Cecile Y. Nierodzinski
Copy Editor: Anne S. Dickson
Designer: Clare T. Minges
Associate Art Director: Cynthia R. Cooper
Illustrator: Kelly Davis
Senior Photographer: John O'Hagan
Photo Stylist: Linda Baltzell Wright
Senior Production Designer: Larry Hunter
Publishing Systems Administrator: Rick Tucker
Production Director: Phillip Lee
Associate Production Manager: Theresa L. Beste
Production Assistant: Faye Porter Bonner

We're Here for You!
We at Oxmoor House are dedicated to serving you with reliable information that expands your imagination and enriches your life. We welcome your comments and suggestions. Please write us at:

Oxmoor House, Inc.
Editor, **Wonder-Under® Book of Easy Appliqué**
2100 Lakeshore Drive
Birmingham, AL 35209

To order additional publications,
call 1-205-877-6560.

C O N

Page 16

Household Wonders

These fusible appliqué projects let you decorate with one eye on style and the other on budget. Bring a touch of the sea into your home with our filmy seashell curtains and table cover (shown above). Use whimsical bird patterns to create a one-of-a-kind headboard for your child's room. Or decorate a wall with the wallhanging in this chapter—it's the bee's knees!

Wearable Wonders

A garment that is slightly worn, a little outdated, or simply too plain and boring will find new life with these quick-and-clever appliqués. Brighten a simple button-front dress (shown below) with a bouquet of spring blossoms. Add a touch of haute couture to your work wardrobe with our elegant suede appliqués. Friends will think you're the cat's meow in one of our black cat Halloween shirts.

Page 48

T E N T S

Childhood Wonders

pages 72–107

Show your children or grandchildren how very special you think they are by showering them with fantastic fusible treasures. She'll be a doll in an appliquéd denim jumper (shown above). Let the moon and stars lull your favorite newborn to sleep when you surround him with our celestial bumper pads. Your kids can travel in style when accompanied by our colorful travel bags.

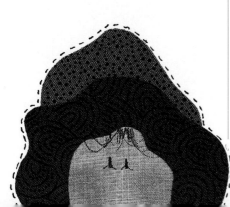

Year-Round Wonders

pages 108–139

Each month holds a reason for celebrating; let Pellon® Wonder-Under® help take the work and worry out of your special-occasion projects. Proclaim the arrival of a new baby with a stork banner (shown below). Set your harvest table with a place mat that gives thanks for all the blessings life has to offer. Create unique Christmas cards with scraps from your fabric bin.

Gift-Giving Wonders

pages 140–160

For the perfect gift for every occasion, look no further. Appliqué a heavenly eyeglass case (shown above) for a friend who has been an angel to you. The case also doubles as a rotary cutter holder! In just a few fast steps, you can create a beautiful anniversary album to present to a special couple. Your favorite sewer will be in stitches when she reads the humorous words written on our pincushion.

Introduction

If you answer yes to any of the five questions below, then fusible appliqué is for you!

• Do you love the look of traditional appliqué, but feel that this time-honored technique does not love you back?

• Do graceful fabric interpretations of flowers, animals, hearts, and stars simply exceed your ability?

• Have you tried every traditional appliqué method from needle-turned to basting and still find turning edges on appliqués to be too hard?

• Do you feel that regardless of what the experts say, freezer paper is not your friend?

• Or do you simply not have the time for all that preparation?

Fusible appliqué is the fast, fun, and practically foolproof solution to any of these problems. You simply substitute paper-backed fusible web for needle and thread. Now, there's nothing you can't appliqué.

Page 115

Pellon® Wonder-Under® is the leading brand of paper-backed fusible web. It has a thin layer of adhesive that, when heated with an iron, fuses layers together. The web is translucent, so you can trace a pattern onto its paper backing. Just trace, press, cut, peel off the backing, and press again. Voilà!—it's appliqué.

You can use Wonder-Under® to fuse fabric to a variety of surfaces, such as fabric, cardboard, paper, or wood. It's pliable, stitchable, washable, and dry-cleanable. (For step-by-step photos that show you how to create fusible appliqué in a few simple steps, see pages 10–11.)

This book is full of appliqué projects made easy. Transform a plain jacket into a custom-designed garment in an hour. Make holiday

decorations without having to start a year in advance. Need a spur-of-the-moment gift? Make a set of note cards in a jiffy. Just add your own special touch with your choice of colors and fabrics.

These project ideas are only the beginning. With Wonder-Under, you can apply any design to almost any project. Although we show seashells on a curtain, you can fuse these designs onto furniture, clothing, or a tote bag. The possibilities are unlimited.

So keep your options open. Sharpen a pencil, fire up the iron, and get ready to appliqué—**the Wonder-Under way.**

To locate a Pellon® Wonder-Under® retailer in your area, call 1-800-223-5275.

Page 52

Appliqué-tions

All the tips and techniques you need to
know to create perfect fusible appliqué are in
this chapter. In addition, we'll show you a variety
of embellishment techniques that add just the right
finishing touch to your appliqué project.

Fusible Facts

Traditional appliqué is the process of sewing fabric shapes onto a background fabric, creating a layered, pictorial design. With fusible appliqué, paper-backed fusible web simplifies this process by replacing the needle and thread. It also creates opportunities to appliqué on materials other than fabric.

Pellon® Wonder-Under® is a paper-backed fusible web, a heat-activated adhesive with a temporary paper lining. A hot iron melts the glue, fusing fabric shapes to the background material. With Wonder-Under, you can fuse any shape in place without sewing a stitch! (However, a finish is sometimes desirable. See Embellishments, page 12.)

In traditional appliqué, turning under fabric edges can be challenging and time-consuming, especially on points, curves, and complex shapes. Wonder-Under eliminates this tedious chore—turning the edge isn't necessary because the web prevents raveling as it holds fabrics in place.

Choose the Correct Weight

Wonder-Under, Regular Weight and Heavy Duty, is available at fabric and craft stores off the bolt or in several prepackaged widths and lengths. It also comes in a ¾"-wide precut tape, 10 yards long, that is ideal for fusing hems and ribbons.

• **Test different weights** to find the Wonder-Under that suits your project. Generally, you can use regular weight web to make wall hangings, curtains, and other soft furnishings. For wood and cardboard applications, a heavy-duty web is preferable. (Heavy Duty Wonder-Under has more glue and therefore more stick.)

• **For a garment,** heavy-duty web may add too much stiffness. Use regular weight web and finish the

appliqué edges as necessary to ensure a washable wearable.

- **For projects in this book,** Regular Weight Wonder-Under is usually recommended unless Heavy Duty is specified.
- **The Wonder-Under package label** gives tips on its application and washability.
- **Test Wonder-Under** on scraps of fabric before you start to appliqué. Let the sample cool, then check to see that the fabric pieces have bonded and the fused layers won't separate.

Experiment with Patterns

Wonder-Under is translucent, so you can lay the web (paper side up) directly on a pattern for tracing. Any printed material or traceable object is a potential pattern. If a tracing or pattern isn't the size you want, use a photocopy machine to enlarge or reduce it.

The following are good pattern sources:

- **Children's books,** coloring books, rubber stamps, greeting cards, and wrapping paper are great pattern sources. Paint stencils, available at most craft stores, are also good for appliqué designs, especially since you can use them to draw directly onto the Wonder-Under paper.
- **Cookie cutters** offer patterns from holiday motifs to a menagerie of animals.
- **Jars, plates, mixing bowls, and teacups** from your kitchen provide an assortment of circles to trace. A small plate with a scalloped edge can make a flower appliqué.
- **Hands, feet, and paws** are potential appliqué patterns, too. So don't forget to look to your children or pets.

Be Careful of Copyright

Be careful how you use designs taken from printed or manufactured items. There's no harm in it, if you use the design only for your own use and enjoyment. However, copyright laws prohibit the use of someone else's design on something you sell or make in quantity, unless you get written permission from the copyright holder. If you plan to sell your work, be sure the appliqué is your own design.

Be Prepared

Fusible appliqué is most fun when you don't encounter an unexpected complication or lack of materials in the middle of a project. Follow these suggestions to make your appliqué experience a pleasant one.

- **Keep these supplies** on hand: fabric marker, iron and ironing board, pressing cloth, scissors (one for paper, another for fabric), and fabrics. And, of course, a sufficient amount of Wonder-Under. For asymmetrical designs, you need tracing paper and a black or red fabric marker.
- **Always prewash** all fabrics to remove sizing, which prevents fusible web from bonding with fabric.
- **Experiment with fabrics.** Cotton works well with fusible appliqué, but you can use more exotic fabrics, too. Be adventurous with lamé, cotton velvet and velveteen, faux suede, or corduroy. Some fabrics require care with application of heat and steam. Be sure to read Step 7 of Fusible Appliqué on page 11 before fusing napped or pile fabrics. Avoid fusing rayon, rayon/acetate, and silk velvet.
- **Use a damp press cloth,** unless otherwise indicated. The press cloth protects your iron and provides moisture to fuse the Wonder-Under to the fabric. It also acts as a temperature and timing guide. After holding the iron on the press cloth for 10–15 seconds, the cloth should be dry. If it is still damp, more time or a higher temperature is needed.

  If a dry press cloth is recommended, you can use brown paper bags, or transparent, silicone-treated pressing paper available at craft stores. You can also use scraps of Wonder-Under release paper from which the web has been removed.
- **Iron on a firm, padded surface.** The padding helps absorb the moisture from the press cloth.
- **Try different backgrounds.** You can use paper, wood, terra-cotta, or any other porous surface. (This book includes some examples.) Be sure the surface is clean and dry before you fuse.
- **Purchase** matching or coordinating thread or fabric paint for finishing the edges of your appliqués. See Embellishments on page 12 for more on finishing.
- **Keep a supply of hot iron cleaner** on hand. Available in most notion departments, the cleaner will remove any Wonder-Under adhesive that may stick to your iron.

Fusible Appliqué

Fusible appliqué is a lot of fun—not a lot of work! Read these general instructions and practice with fabric scraps before starting a project.

1 If an appliqué pattern has a **symmetrical (balanced)** design, trace the pattern onto the paper (smooth) side of the Wonder-Under. (The adhesive side has a rougher texture.) Leaving a margin around the shape, use paper scissors to cut out the design.

3 Place the adhesive (rough) side of the web on the wrong side of the appliqué fabric. Press for 5–8 seconds with a hot, dry iron. Do not overheat. If desired, use a dry pressing cloth between the iron and the appliqué to avoid getting adhesive on the iron.

2 If an appliqué pattern has an **asymmetrical (one-way)** design, the finished appliqué will be a mirror image of the pattern. So if a pattern points left, the appliqué will point right. In this book, patterns are reversed as needed (which is why the pattern on page 119 looks like ဝဝ၉ instead of Boo). For patterns that are not reversed, copy the design onto tracing paper, and darken the image on both sides of the paper. Trace the wrong side of the drawing onto the Wonder-Under. Leaving a margin around the shape, cut out the piece.

4 Let the fabric cool completely. Then use fabric scissors to cut out the motif along the drawn line. If desired, use pinking shears for a decorative edge.

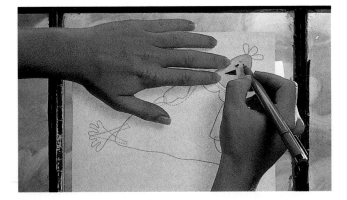

5 To mark detail or embroidery lines, place the cut-out piece over the reversed pattern, and lightly trace lines onto the right side of the fabric. If you can't see the pattern through the fabric, use a light box, or tape a tracing of the design onto a windowpane to let the sun illuminate the pattern.

7 With the web side down, position the appliqué on the right side of the background material. When sure of the placement, cover the appliqué with a damp press cloth. Press firmly for 10–15 seconds with the iron on wool setting. (Heavy fabrics may require a little more time.) Remove the press cloth and iron the project to eliminate excess moisture. Let the fabric cool.

Napped or pile fabrics, such as velvet, corduroy, and terry cloth require special handling. Fuse appliqués made from these fabrics from the wrong side of the background fabric. Baste or pin the appliqué on the right side of the background fabric along one edge. Place the appliqué facedown on a terry cloth towel, scrap of pile fabric, or needleboard, and fuse from the wrong side. This method may require more fusing time. To finish, machine satin-stitch the edges.

6 Peel off the paper backing. An easy way to get an edge to peel is to begin tearing the Wonder-Under release paper. This will immediately lift up an edge.

8 Where appliqués overlap, start fusing the pieces in the back of the design, and work up to the front, or topmost, pieces. If one piece is layered atop another (like the chicken's beak above), cut out the base shape, but do not peel away the protective paper. Lightly fuse the second piece in place on the base. Peel the paper off the base piece, and use full heat to fuse the combined appliqué in place.

Embellishment Techniques

The simplicity of fusible appliqué is part of its appeal. But additional details, or embellishments, add a finishing touch that can be beautiful and personal. Embellishment can also be functional. Pellon® Wonder-Under® holds appliqués securely in place, but some fraying can occur with frequent use. On such projects, consider adding a finish to fabric appliqués. Here are some ideas and techniques for embellishment that will enhance your fusible appliqué.

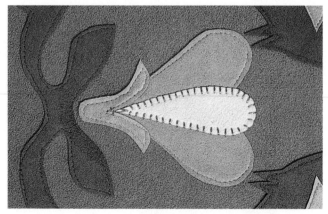

2 A decorative, open zigzag stitch is also fast and easy to machine-sew and adds security to edges. Closely spaced zigzag stitches, or satin stitch, give shapes strong definition and completely encase raw edges. Machine satin stitch requires practice and skill to stitch corners, points, and curves. You can work satin stitch by hand, but it is very time-consuming.

1 A machine-sewn topstitch provides an extra measure of security, permanently holding the edge of an appliqué in place. Use contrasting or matching thread or invisible monofilament thread to outline the shape close to the edge with a straight machine stitch.

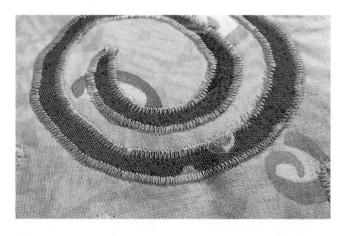

3 A hand-embroidered buttonhole stitch is a pretty edging that adds color, texture, and character to your work. Consider other embroidery stitches, too, such as French knots and lazy daisy stitches.

4 You can also glue or topstitch rickrack, braid, lace, or other trims around an appliqué to give it extra dimension and color.

6 Fine-tipped fabric markers are an easy way to add detail to appliqués. After cutting out an appliqué, place it over the pattern to trace details directly onto the fabric. To make a pattern easier to see, use a light box, or tape the pattern to a bright windowpane. You can also use fine-tip markers to draw "quilting lines" around the edges of an appliqué. This technique is sometimes called pen stitching.

5 Another popular no-sew finish is washable fabric paint. Available at craft stores, these paints come in squeeze tubes that allow you to apply a thin line of paint around an appliqué. Insert cardboard under the appliqué to prevent seepage. Follow the manufacturer's directions for drying time—some paints require several days to set. Most manufacturers recommend washing the finished project in warm water.

7 Buttons and beads add dimension and sparkle to any appliqué. Sewn or glued in place, they can represent flower centers, snow, and other details.

page 39

page 41

page 26

Household Wonders

Whether you want to freshen your
home decor or go for a completely
different look, this chapter has just
what you are looking for. You'll find
appliqués to brighten every room in your
house—from the bedroom to the study.

Seaside Sheers

Fusible appliqué provides you with a sea of decorating possibilities. Inexpensive sheer white curtains look custom-made with seashell appliqués in a palette of sherbet colors. Washable fabric paint finishes the appliquéd edges of the matching tablecloth.

materials

For both

3 yards Pellon® Wonder-Under®

½ yard each 5 pastel fabrics

For sheers

1 pair purchased sheer curtains

For tablecloth

70"-diameter purchased tablecloth

Pearlized dimensional fabric paint in coordinating colors

Curtain Instructions

1. Trace shell patterns onto paper side of Wonder-Under. You will need at least 30 assorted shells to cover a two-panel curtain. Leaving approximately ½" margin, cut around each shape.
2. Referring to Appliqué-tions on page 10, press Wonder-Under shapes onto fabric scraps. Cut out fabric shapes along pattern lines.
3. Remove paper backing from each piece.
4. Position shells on right side of each curtain panel, arranging pieces until you achieve a pleasing balance of color and shape. (For a softer look, place shells on wrong side of curtain panels. Even with transfer web applied, fabrics will show through, although they will appear muted. Curtains shown are made in this manner.)
5. When satisfied with placement, fuse shells in place.

Tablecloth Instructions

1. Trace 50 waves and at least 25 assorted shells onto paper side of Wonder-Under. Leaving approximately ½" margin, cut around each shape.
2. Referring to Appliqué-tions on page 10, press Wonder-Under shape onto wrong side of fabric scraps. Cut out fabric shapes along pattern lines.
3. Remove paper backing from fabric pieces.
4. Fold tablecloth in half, then in quarters to find center. Measure 12" from center point along each fold line to define center circle of tablecloth. Use pins to mark perimeter of center circle that will rest on top of table.
5. Position shells close together inside center circle. Scatter remaining shells outside center circle. Position waves around bottom edge of tablecloth. When satisfied with placement, remove pins and fuse all pieces in place.

6. Outline shells and waves with fabric paint. Leave tablecloth flat until completely dry.

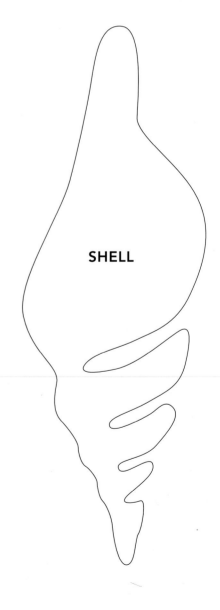

SHELL

Designed by Carol Tipton

SHELLS

WAVE

18

Celestial Bolster Pillow

Designed by Peggy Ann Williams

If you have ever wished for the sun, moon, and stars, you'll find this pillow to be just heavenly. Each of three sections is filled with its own pillow form, giving the bolster the illusion of throw pillows in one elongated form.

materials

Paper to make bolster pillow pattern

2 yards 54"-wide decorator fabric for bolster

¼ yard Pellon® Wonder-Under®

¼ yard coordinating decorator fabric for appliqués

Thread to match appliqué fabric (optional)

6 yards cording with ½"-wide lip

3 (12" x 16") pillow forms

Instructions

Finished Size: Approximately 16" x 33"

Note: Seam allowances are ½".

1. To make paper bolster pattern, referring to Diagram A, draw a 16" x 37" rectangle. For ties, draw one 3" x 11" extension at each corner. Mark ½" seam allowances along all pattern edges. Divide rectangle into three vertical sections, each 12" wide.

2. For bolster front, transfer pattern to decorator fabric. Mark vertical section lines. Cut out. For

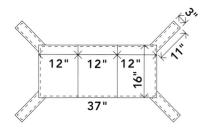

Diagram A

bolster back, referring to diagrams B and C on page 20, cut two pieces from decorator fabric, omitting lower extensions on top back piece and upper extensions on bottom back piece. Mark two vertical section lines on each piece.

STAR

3. To hem top back piece (piece with upper extensions), fold lower straight edge under ½" and press. Fold under again 2" and press. Stitch along first fold.

4. For bottom back piece (piece with lower extensions), with wrong sides facing, fold fabric in half horizontally. Machine-baste along side and bottom edges of rectangle area.

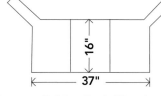

Diagram B (Top Back Piece)

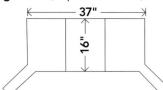

Diagram C (Bottom Back Piece)

5. Referring to Diagram D, with right sides faceup, place bottom back piece on top of top back piece, aligning edges to form a 16" x 37" rectangle. Pin sides. Machine-baste. Set aside.

6. Trace sun, moon, and star patterns onto paper side of Wonder-Under. Mark shaded swirl on sun pattern. Leaving approximately ½" margin, cut around each shape.

20

SUN

Diagram D

16"

37"

Do not cut out shaded swirl. Referring to Appliqué-tions on page 10, press shapes onto wrong side of appliqué fabric. Cut out shapes. Cut out shaded area on sun. Center and fuse one fabric shape to each section of bolster front. If desired for added security, using short stitch length and narrow width, zigzag-stitch around cut edges of appliqués.

7. With fabric edges and cording lip aligned, machine-baste cording to right side of bolster front.

8. With right sides facing and edges aligned, pin bolster front to bolster back. Stitch along all edges, including extensions. Trim seam allowances and clip curves; turn. Press. Pin front and back together along section lines; top-stitch along section lines.

9. Insert one pillow form into each section. Tie each extension into knot.

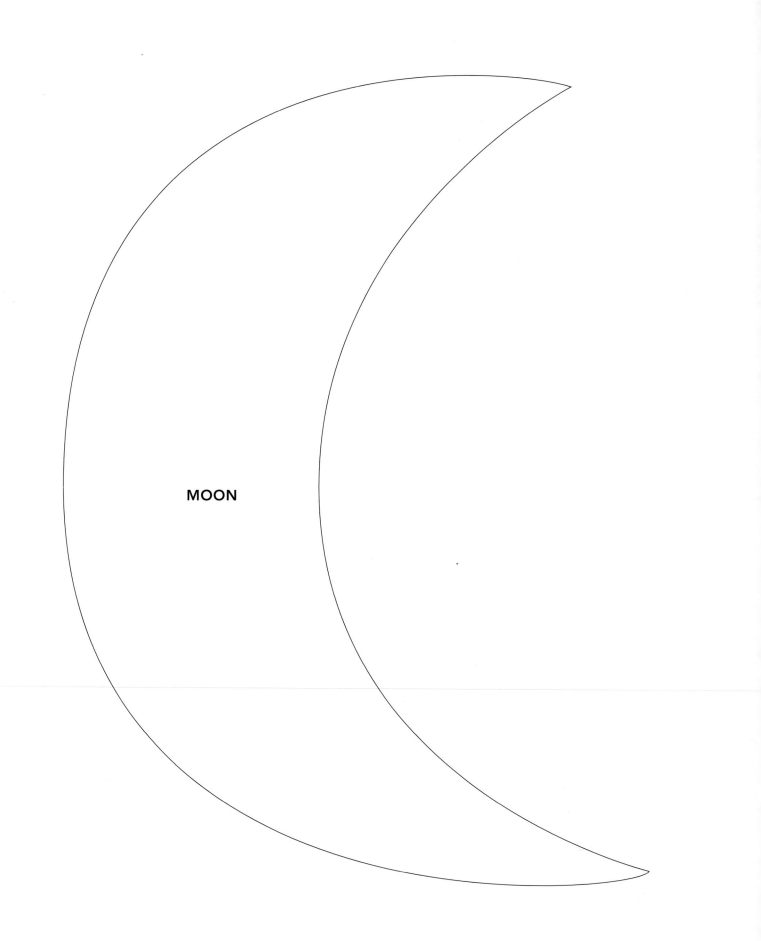

MOON

Blanket Statement

Understated elegance is the hallmark of this wool blanket bordered by an appliquéd turnback. The technique used to create this edging is easy, and the result is simply exquisite. Any bride and groom would treasure this gift. Once complete, however, you will likely want to keep it for yourself!

materials

Purchased wool blanket

Seam ripper

10" square of paper, folded in half

2⅝ yards Pellon® Wonder-Under®

1½ yards lightweight tear-away stabilizer

2 large spools thread to match blanket

Instructions

Note: To avoid shrinkage after appliquéing, dry-clean blanket before you begin.

1. Using seam ripper, remove binding from one end of blanket.

2. Transfer palm leaf pattern to folded piece of paper and cut out.

3. From Wonder-Under, cut one 10"-wide strip equal in length to width of blanket.

4. Fold Wonder-Under strip in half with short sides together to find center. To figure number of pattern repeats, divide width of blanket (in inches) by nine. Referring to Diagram and beginning at center of paper side of Wonder-Under strip, trace palm leaf design an equal number of times to left and right of center. (If your blanket does not divide evenly, trace leaves further apart to accommodate blanket's dimensions.) Do not cut out design.

5. With edges aligned and palm leaf tip closest to raw edge, refer to Appliqué-tions on page 10 to press Wonder-Under onto right side of blanket. Trim palm leaves along pattern lines. Remove paper backing.

6. Fold Wonder-Under onto blanket along straight bottom edge, sandwiching Wonder-Under between blanket layers and creating finished edge. Fuse blanket layers together.

7. Cut two 10"-wide strips of stabilizer, and pin end-to-end to underside of blanket behind design area. Trim any excess.

8. With matching thread, satin-stitch raw edges of leaf design, using stitch slightly larger than medium width. Straightstitch area at outer side edges closed. Following manufacturer's instructions, remove excess stabilizer. Press.

other ideas

Transform a plain tablecloth into an heirloom linen by applying this graceful edging. Be sure to purchase a tablecloth larger than the size you need. Adding this border to both long edges will reduce the width of your tablecloth by about 19". You will need to shorten the length accordingly. This appliqué technique looks equally lovely adorning the edge of an oversized bath towel. Simply reduce the size of the palm leaf pattern on a photocopier to fit your towel.

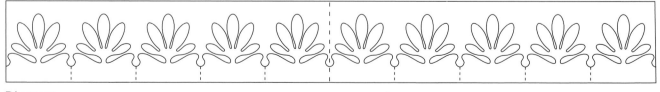

Diagram

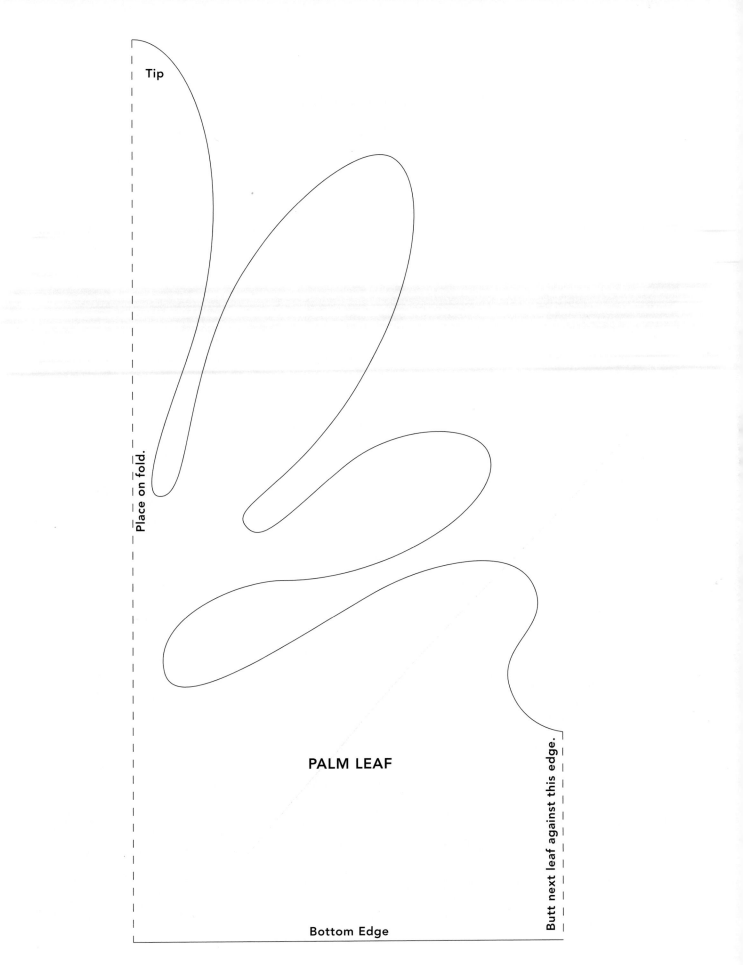

Tip

Place on fold.

PALM LEAF

Butt next leaf against this edge.

Bottom Edge

Bee's Knees

With more than 20 different appliqué motifs designed with incredible attention to detail, this wall hanging truly is the bee's knees! Assemble all the appliqués as we did here for a most enchanting quiltlet, or select a few of your favorites to embellish a variety of purchased items. The possibilities are endless!

materials

⅓ yard dark green solid fabric for sashing and leaves

7 different beige tone-on-tone background fabrics: 1 (13½" x 10¼"), 1 (14¼" x 10¼"), 1 (7½" x 10¼"), 1 (9¼" x 10¼"), 1 (16½" x 15½"), 1 (11¼" x 19¼"), and 1 (11¼" x 6½")

2 yards Pellon® Wonder-Under®

¼ yard medium green solid fabric for leaves

¼ yard light green solid fabric for leaves

⅓ yard white tone-on-tone fabric

¼ yard gold tone-on-tone fabric for bees

Assorted scraps for appliqués

Black fine-tip permanent fabric marker

Powdered blusher

1 yard backing fabric

30" x 38" thin quilt batting

Yellow seed beads

Buttons: 3 (¼")ladybugs, 2 (¼") stars, assorted round flat, 2 (⅛"-diameter) round white, 1 heart-in-hand, and 2 (¼") black shank*

Ecru pearl cotton

Embroidery needle

1 keyring charm*

Black quilting thread

4 yards purchased green extra-wide double-fold bias tape for binding

6" x 30" length muslin for hanging sleeve

*If you prefer, substitute any novelty button or charm shape for those listed.

Instructions
Finished Size: 28" x 36"

Note: Seam allowances are ¼". Dashes on patterns indicate lines of underlying pattern pieces.

1. For sashing, cut the following lengths from dark green solid fabric: two ¾" x 10¼", one ¾" x 27½", one ¾" x 16½", one ¾" x 11¼", and one ¾ x 25".

2. Referring to Assembly Diagram on page 28, join background blocks using designated sashing strips. Press all seams toward sashing strips.

3. From fabric for girl's dress, cut one 1" x 5" strip. Referring to Appliqué-tions on page 10, press Wonder-Under onto wrong side of all remaining fabrics except binding and backing fabrics. Press Wonder-Under onto *right* side of 1" x 5" dress fabric strip.

4. Upper left block: To apply appliqués, referring to detail photo on page 29 for colors, trace one lower branch, one upper branch, one bird on branch, two medium bees, 14 large tree leaves, and six small tree leaves onto paper side of Wonder-Under. Cut out shapes along pattern lines. Remove paper backing. Fuse upper branch, lower branch, and tree leaves in place. Referring to pattern, fuse bird in place in order indicated on pattern. Fuse bee pieces in place in order indicated. Referring to detail photo and using black fabric marker, add pen stitching and details.

5. Upper right block: To apply appliqués, referring to detail photo on page 29 for colors, trace one hat, two medium bees, two round flowers, eight four-petal flowers, seven small flower leaves, and five large flower leaves onto paper side of Wonder-Under. Cut out shapes along pattern lines. Remove paper backing. Fuse hat pieces in place on block in order indicated on pattern. Fuse four-petal flowers, small flower leaves, round flowers, large flower leaves, and medium bee pieces in place, respectively. Referring to detail photo and using black fabric marker, add pen stitching and details.

6. Middle right block: To apply appliqués, referring to detail photo on page 30 for colors, trace one pot, one flying bird, one ladybug, four large tulips, one wavy oval flower, one wavy round flower, two medium bees, four large flower leaves, and three ¼" x 2" stems onto paper side of Wonder-Under. Cut out shapes along pattern lines. Remove paper backing. Referring to detail photo, fuse stems in place. Fuse pot and lady-bug in place in order indicated. (Do not fuse flying bird yet.) Fuse large tulips, wavy oval flower, wavy round flower, and large flower leaves in place, respectively, over-lapping as desired. Fuse medium bees in place in order indicated. Referring to detail photo and using black fabric marker, add pen stitch-ing, ladybug head, and details.

7. Lower right block: To apply appliqués, referring to detail photo on page 30 for colors, trace one tree, one bird under tree, one girl, two medium bees, eight small tree leaves, four daisy leaves, eight daisies, one ⅛" x 2" stem, two ⅛" x 1" stems, and one daisy petal (use small tree leaf pattern) onto paper side of Wonder-Under. (Note: Cut light blue shaded pat-tern piece from 1" x 5" fabric strip to which Wonder-Under has been fused to right side.) Cut out shapes along pattern lines. Remove paper backing. Referring to detail photo,

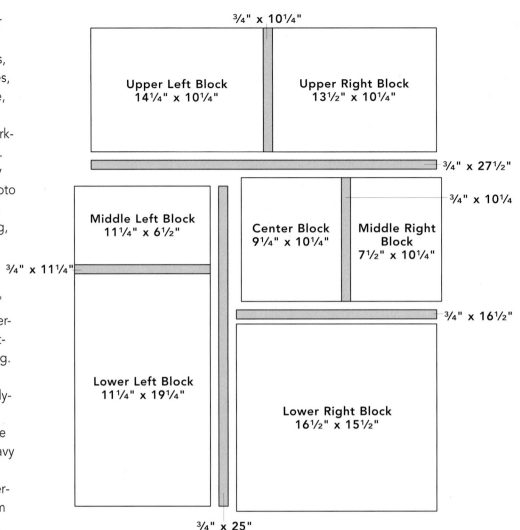

¾" x 10¼"

Upper Left Block
14¼" x 10¼"

Upper Right Block
13½" x 10¼"

¾" x 27½"

¾" x 10¼"

Middle Left Block
11¼" x 6½"

¾" x 11¼"

Center Block
9¼" x 10¼"

Middle Right Block
7½" x 10¼"

¾" x 16½"

Lower Left Block
11¼" x 19¼"

Lower Right Block
16½" x 15½"

¾" x 25"

Assembly Diagram

fuse tree, flying bird, and tree leaves in place respectively. Fuse bird under tree in place in order indicated. Fuse ⅛" x 2" stem and ⅛" x 1" stems in place. Referring to pattern, fuse girl in place in order indicated. Fuse daisy leaves and daisies in place respectively. Fuse medium bees in place in order indicated. Referring to detail photo and using black fabric marker, add pen stitching and details. Using powdered blusher, add cheeks and knees to girl.

8. Lower left block: To apply appliqués, referring to detail photo on page 30 for colors, trace one

tall birdhouse, one birdhouse with cats, one birdhouse with heart, one birdhouse with large roof, one fence, one grass, two vines, two medium bees, two small bees, 32 vine leaves, 11 small tulips, one ¼" x 13½" birdhouse post, one ¼" x 9½" birdhouse post, and one ¼" x 11½" birdhouse post onto paper side of Wonder-Under. Cut out shapes along pattern lines. Remove paper backing. Fuse bird-house posts in place. Referring to pattern, fuse birdhouses (and one small bee on top of birdhouse) in place in order indicated. Position cat on block. Do not fuse. Position

28

Upper Left Block

Upper Right Block

fence on block. Do not fuse. Referring to photo, pull tail, head, and front leg of cat through to top of fence. Fuse fence and cat in place. Fuse grass, vines, and vine leaves in place. Fuse small tulips and leaves in place, overlapping as desired. Fuse remaining small bee and medium bees in place in order indicated on medium bee pattern.

Referring to detail photo and using black fabric marker, add pen stitching, ladybug heads, and details.

9. Middle left block: To apply appliqués, referring to detail photo on page 30 for colors, trace one cat head, one cat tail, two medium bees, one round flower, four wavy oval flowers, one large tulip, and three large flower leaves onto

paper side of Wonder-Under. Cut out shapes along pattern lines. Remove paper backing. Fuse cat head, large tulip, large flower leaves, round flower, and all but one wavy oval flower in place, overlapping as desired. Fuse cat tail in place. Fuse remaining wavy oval flower in place, covering straight end of cat tail. Referring to photo and using black fabric marker, add pen stitching and details.

10. Center block: To apply appliqués, referring to detail photo on page 30 for colors, trace one bee with legs and eight daisies onto paper side of Wonder-Under. Cut out shapes along pattern lines. Remove paper backing. Fuse bee with legs in place in order indicated. Fuse daisies in place. Referring to photo and using black fabric marker, add pen stitching and details.

11. To apply border leaf appliqués, using solid dark green, solid medium green, and solid light green fabrics, trace 50 border leaves (use daisy leaf pattern) onto paper side of Wonder-Under. Cut out shapes along lines. Remove paper backing. Fuse leaves on sashing strips. Referring to photo and using black fabric marker, add pen stitching and veins.

12. Layer backing fabric (facedown), batting, and wall hanging top (faceup). Hand-baste layers together. Using sewing thread, sew three seed beads in center of each daisy, stitching through all layers.

13. Thread embroidery needle with pearl cotton, but do not knot. Referring to detail photo of upper left block, position one ladybug button on lower branch. Working from top of button, run needle down into one hole in button.

Middle Right Block

Lower Right Block

Middle Left Block

Lower Left Block

Center Block

Bring needle up through opposite hole, catching all layers. Tie ends of pearl cotton in tight double knot over button. Trim pearl cotton, leaving short tails.

14. Referring to Step 13 and detail photo of upper right block, use pearl cotton to tie one star button and four round flat buttons in centers of four-petal flowers. Referring to detail photo of middle right block, tie one ladybug button in place. Referring to detail photo of lower right block, tie ⅛" white buttons in place on girl's shoes. Referring to detail photo of lower left block, tie one ladybug button on one birdhouse post; tie one round flat button in center of tall birdhouse and in center of birdhouse with large roof; and tie heart-in-hand button to sashing.

15. Referring to detail photo of middle right block and using sewing thread, sew keyring charm in beak of bird, stitching through all layers. Referring to photo of center block, sew one black shank button in center of each bee leg, stitching through all layers. For cat whiskers, thread needle with doubled black quilting thread. Referring to Step 13, tie whiskers on all cats in lower left block.

16. To bind wall hanging, machine-baste layers together ¼" from edge. Trim batting and backing fabric even with wall hanging. With right sides facing, raw edges aligned, pin bias tape to front, beginning at midpoint of one side of wall hanging. Stitch bias tape along one edge of wall hanging, sewing through all layers and backstitching at beginning of seam. Stitch to seam line at corner; backstitch. Lift presser foot and turn wall hanging to stitch along next edge. Continue stitching in this manner. Join ends of bias tape by overlapping and stitching by hand. Turn bias tape to back of wall hanging and blindstitch in place. At each corner, fold excess bias tape neatly and blindstitch in place. Remove hand-basted stitches.

17. To make hanging sleeve, turn under ¼" on short ends of muslin; press. Turn under 1" more; press. Topstitch. With wrong sides facing, stitch long edges together. Press seam allowance open, centering seam on one side of tube. With sleeve seam facing wall hanging back, place sleeve just below binding at top edge, centering it between sides. Slipstitch top and bottom edges of sleeve to quilt backing only, making sure no stitches go through to front. Slip dowel or curtain rod through sleeve. Hang from brackets on wall.

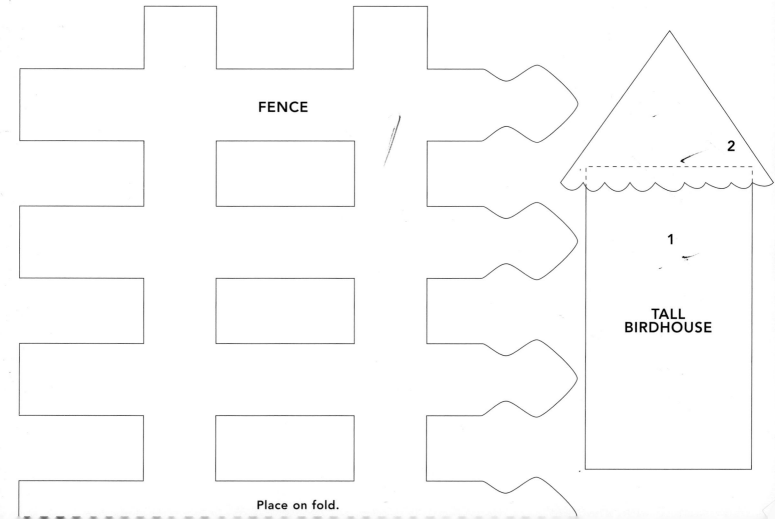

FENCE

TALL BIRDHOUSE

2

1

Place on fold.

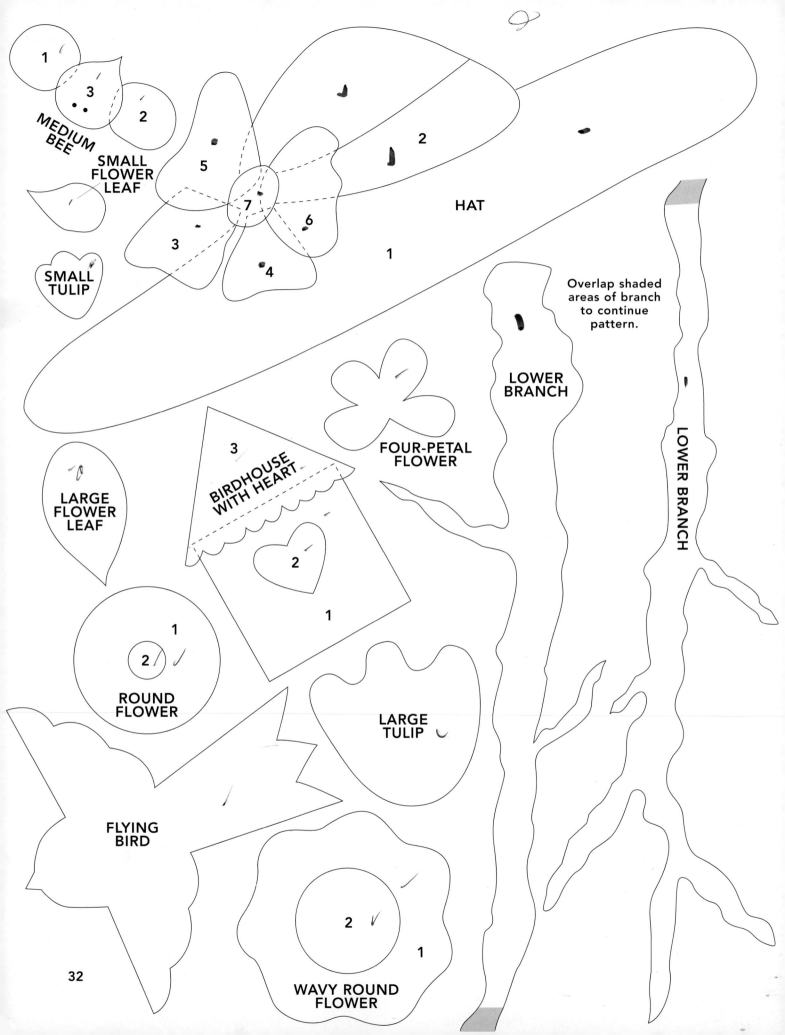

MEDIUM
BEE

SMALL
FLOWER
LEAF

SMALL
TULIP

HAT

Overlap shaded
areas of branch
to continue
pattern.

LOWER
BRANCH

LOWER BRANCH

LARGE
FLOWER
LEAF

BIRDHOUSE
WITH HEART

FOUR-PETAL
FLOWER

ROUND
FLOWER

LARGE
TULIP

FLYING
BIRD

32

WAVY ROUND
FLOWER

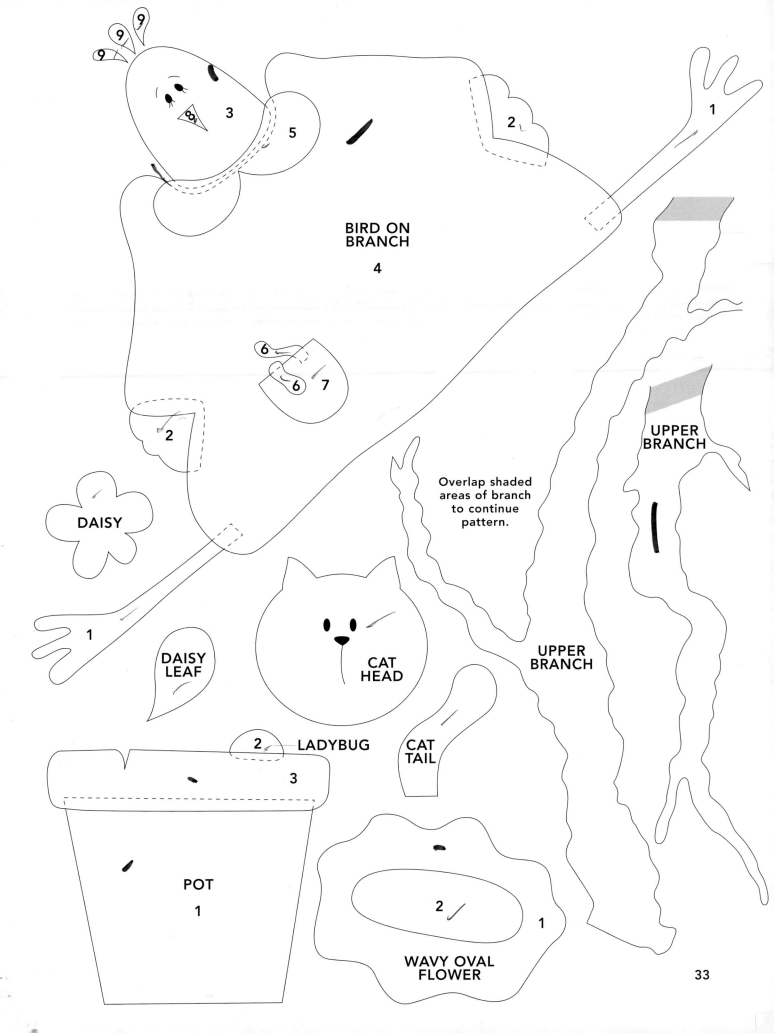

BIRD ON
BRANCH

4

3

5

2

1

9
9
9

2

6
6
7

DAISY

Overlap shaded
areas of branch
to continue
pattern.

UPPER
BRANCH

1

DAISY
LEAF

CAT
HEAD

UPPER
BRANCH

CAT
TAIL

2   LADYBUG

3

POT

1

2

1

WAVY OVAL
FLOWER

33

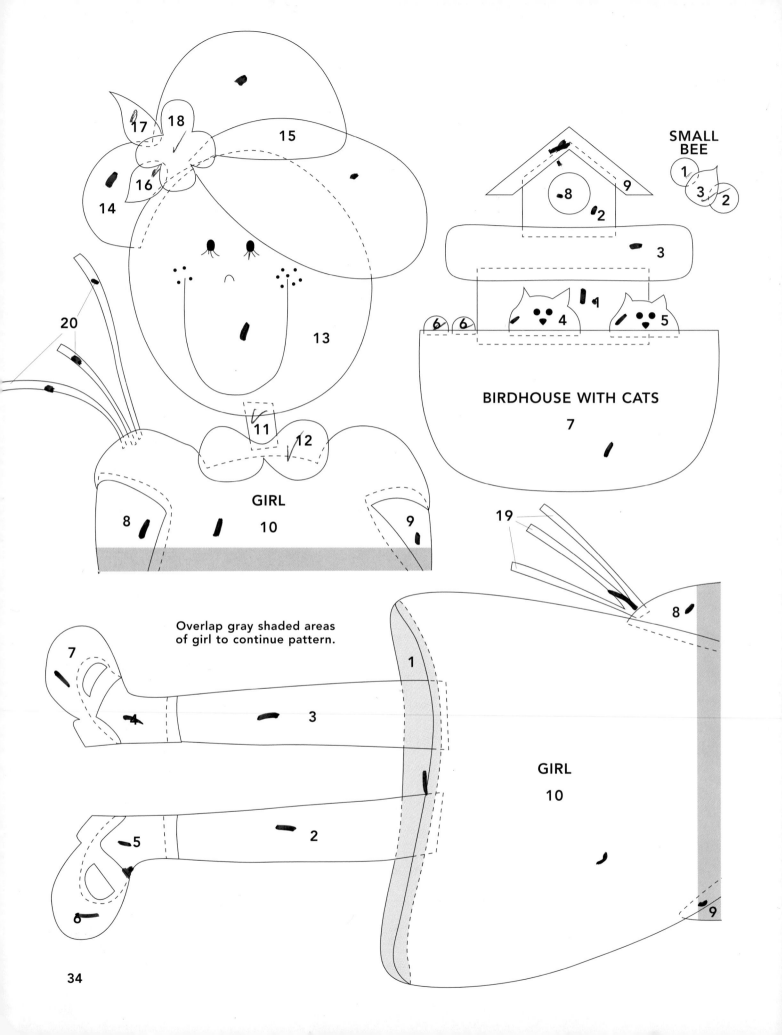

SMALL
BEE

BIRDHOUSE WITH CATS

7

GIRL

10

GIRL

10

Overlap gray shaded areas
of girl to continue pattern.

34

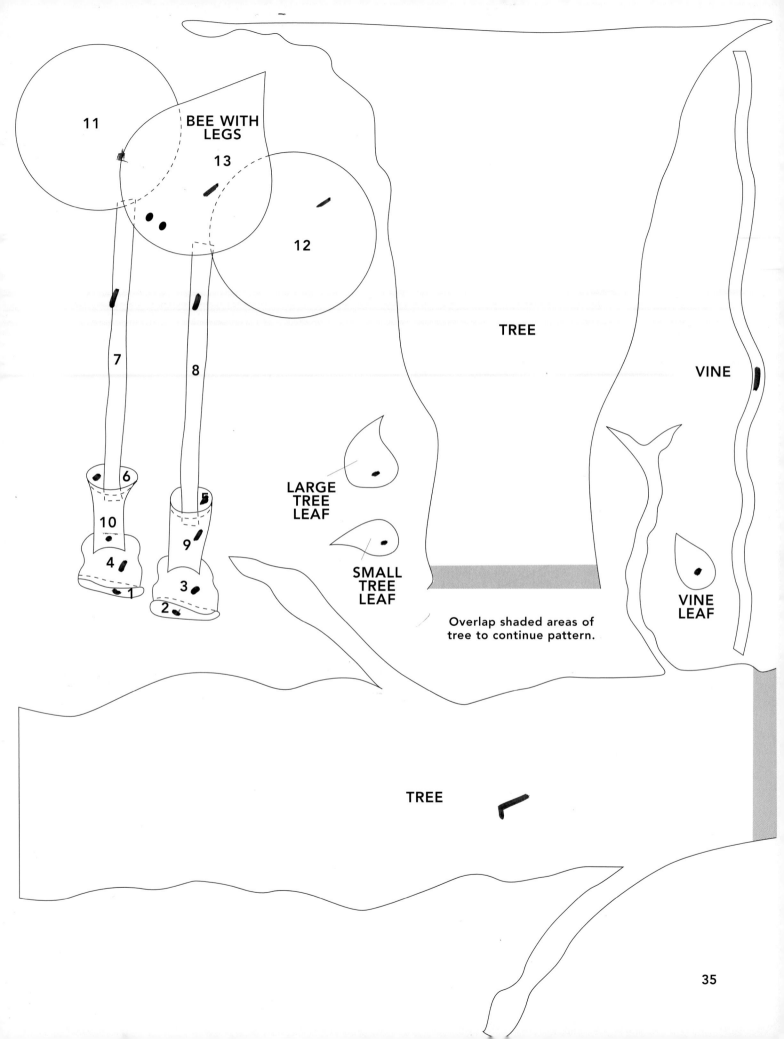

BEE WITH
LEGS

11

13

12

7

8

6

10

5

9

4

1

2

3

TREE

VINE

LARGE
TREE
LEAF

SMALL
TREE
LEAF

Overlap shaded areas of
tree to continue pattern.

VINE
LEAF

TREE

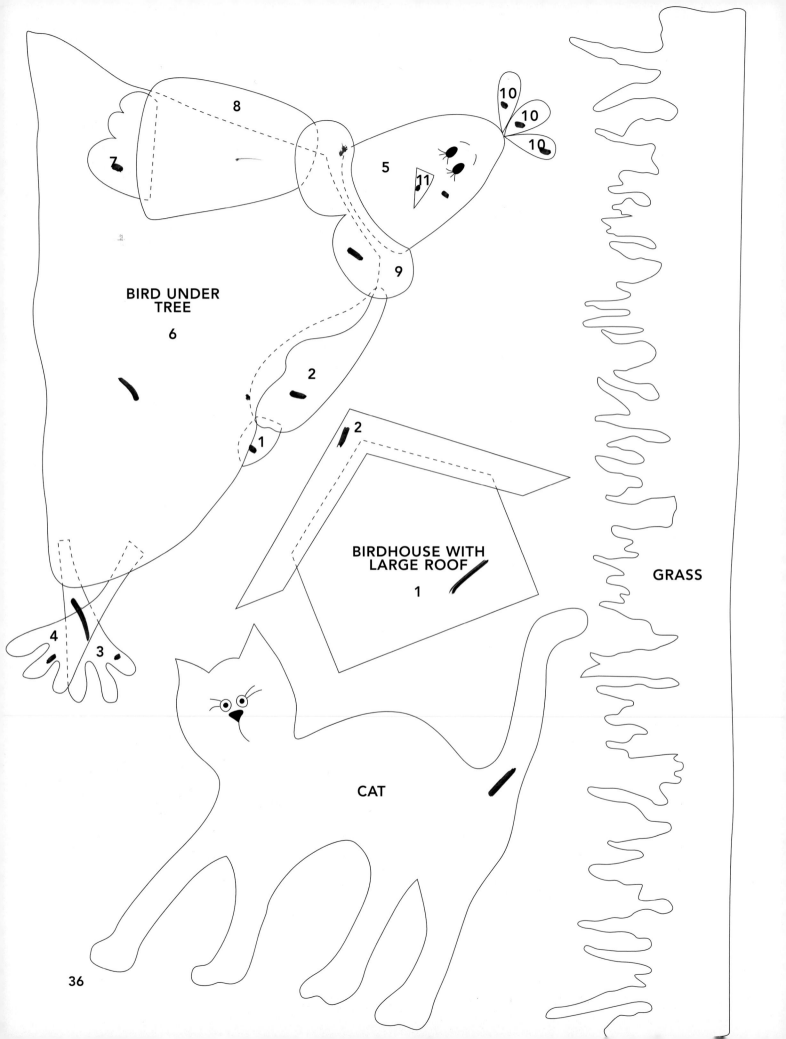

BIRD UNDER
TREE

6

8

7

10
10
10

5

11

9

2

1

BIRDHOUSE WITH
LARGE ROOF

2

1

4

3

GRASS

CAT

36

It's a Frame-up

Designed by Carol Tipton

This mirror appeals to both the budget-minded and the style conscious. While it looks like you might find it at a pricey art gallery, you can make it from the most inexpensive of materials—a discount store mirror, cardboard, and fabric scraps.

materials

Purchased mirror in plain, flat wooden frame

Single-edge razor blade

Regular thick cardboard

Corrugated cardboard

Hot-glue gun and glue sticks

Heavy Duty Pellon® Wonder-Under®

Fabric scraps: black, brick red, gold miniprint, turquoise

Instructions

Note: Use a dry press cloth for this project.

1. Using purchased mirror as a guide and referring to photo, use razor blade to cut one 2½"-wide frame and one 4¾"-wide frame from regular cardboard. From corrugated cardboard, cut one 4¾"-wide frame. Hot-glue corrugated frame, ridge side up, on top of corresponding regular cardboard frame. Set aside.

2. Referring to Appliqué-tions on page 10, press Wonder-Under onto wrong side of fabric scraps. Trace pattern shapes onto paper side of Wonder-Under. Cut out shapes along pattern outlines. Remove paper backing. Referring to photo, arrange fabric shapes on smaller regular cardboard frame. Fuse in place.

3. With opening edges aligned, hot-glue smaller frame onto larger corrugated-covered frame.

4. Cut 1½" squares from corrugated cardboard scraps. Cut each square in half diagonally. Referring to photo, offset triangles to form "open" squares, and arrange them around outer edge of corrugated frame. Hot-glue triangles in place.

5. Hot-glue cardboard frame to mirror frame.

other ideas

Tie your whole room together by applying appliqués to a variety of home dec items. Fuse appliqués to a flat wooden picture frame or around the rim of a smooth lamp shade.

hottip
clean up

Even if you use a press cloth, stray fibers of adhesive may stick to your iron. Have no fear—there are several brands of iron cleaners available that will remove the adhesive. The cleaners, sold in tubes, are found in the notions section of your fabric store. In addition to fusible adhesive, these cleaners remove spray starch and other buildup.

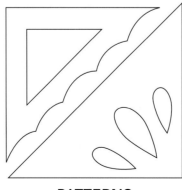

PATTERNS

Stars & Stripes

Designed by Carol Tipton

Bring a touch of Old Glory into your home with this rustic trunk
and matching floorcloth. The classic look of stars and stripes is a decorating favorite,
and these fusible appliqués make the effect easy to achieve.

materials

For both

3"-wide paintbrush

2 yards Heavy Duty Pellon® Wonder-Under®

Fabric: ¼ yard white cotton, ½ yard blue star print cotton, ¾ yard red-and-cream plaid cotton

For trunk

Unfinished 35" x 14" x 18½" wooden trunk

Sandpaper

Semigloss varnish

For floorcloth

6 yards ¾"-wide Pellon® Wonder-Under® fusible tape

34" x 54" piece heavyweight cotton canvas

Newspaper

1 quart cream latex semi-gloss enamel paint

Acrylic paint: 1 bottle each golden, white

Paper plate

Sponge

Trunk Instructions

Finished Size: 35" x 14" x 18½"

Note: Use a dry press cloth for this project.

1. Sand and varnish wooden trunk. Let dry.

2. Trace 11 stars onto paper side of Wonder-Under. Leaving approximately ½" margin, cut around each shape.

3. Referring to Appliqué-tions on page 10, press Wonder-Under

shapes onto wrong side of white fabric. Cut out fabric shapes along pattern lines. Remove the paper backing and set aside.

4. Press Wonder-Under onto wrong side of blue star print. Draw 11 (3") squares on paper side of Wonder-Under and cut out. Do not remove paper backing.

5. Press Wonder-Under onto wrong side of red-and-cream plaid. Draw two parallel lines 7" apart on paper side of Wonder-Under. Referring to Diagram, cut approximately ½"-wide wavy strips between parallel lines. Remove paper backing. Set strips aside.

6. Center one white star faceup on right side of each blue square. Fuse stars in place. Remove paper backing from squares. Position three squares in a row on center of lid, spacing evenly. Position two sets of three wavy strips between squares. Fuse appliqués to lid.

7. Turn trunk on its back so that trunk front is faceup. Referring to photo, position squares and strips on trunk front. Fuse appliqués in place.

Floorcloth Instructions

Finished Size: 30" x 50"

1. To hem floorcloth, press fusible tape onto one side of canvas piece along each long edge. Remove paper backing. Turn long edges under 2" and fuse hem in place. Press fusible tape onto short edges of canvas piece, overlapping hemmed ends of long edges. Turn short edges under 2" and fuse hem in place.

2. Cover large, flat surface with newspaper. Place canvas piece

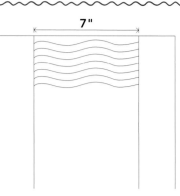

Diagram

faceup on newspaper. Paint right side of canvas with three coats of latex enamel paint. Let dry between coats.

3. Pour large puddle of golden acrylic paint onto paper plate. Squeeze swirl of white acrylic paint on top of golden paint. Dip sponge into paints, allowing colors to mix on sponge. Sponge-paint right side of canvas, reloading sponge as necessary. Let paint dry for 24 hours.

4. Refer to steps 2–4 for trunk to trace and cut out 15 white stars and 15 blue squares.

5. Refer to Step 5 for trunk to make wavy strips.

6. Center one white star faceup on right side of each blue square. Fuse stars in place. Remove paper backing from squares. Referring to photo and working on one small section at a time, position squares and wavy strips on canvas and fuse in place.

STAR

Birds of a Feather

A child's room should be fun and whimsical—just like these delightfully silly birds. They are as playful as a child's imagination. The appliqués are a quick embellishment to an easy-to-assemble headboard kit. When finished, your child will love the way you feathered her nest.

materials

Custom headboard kit*

Black-and-white check fabric
(Twin: 34" x 48", Full: 34"
x 66", Queen: 34" x 72",
King: 34" x 92")

Masking tape

2 yards Pellon® Wonder-
Under®

Small print fabric: ¼ yard
each: yellow, orange, red,
purple, blue, and green;
scraps light gray

Thread to match fabrics
(optional)

5 (¼") black buttons

Straight pins

Staple gun (optional)

1⅝ yard ⅜"-wide orange
grosgrain ribbon

2⅔ yards ⅜"-wide yellow
grosgrain ribbon

Hot-glue gun and glue sticks

Permanent black fabric marker

* For information on where to
purchase a custom headboard
kit, contact Cynthia East
Fabrics, 1523 Rebsamen Park
Road, Little Rock, AR 72202;
(501) 663-0460, fax (501)
663-1514

Instructions

1. Following manufacturer's instructions, assemble headboard and attach foam.

2. Press black-and-white check fabric. Center fabric on foam-covered headboard. Mark outline of headboard with masking tape. Remove fabric.

3. Trace pattern pieces onto paper side of Wonder-Under. For each bird, trace one body, one beak, one tail, one inner eye, one outer eye, three head feathers, and three tail feathers. Leaving ¼" margin, cut around each shape. Referring to Appliqué-tions on page 10 and referring to photo for colors, press Wonder-Under shapes onto wrong side of corresponding fabrics. Cut out shapes along pattern lines. Remove paper backings.

4. Referring to photo, position fabric shapes on right side of black-and-white check fabric in marked area. Fuse in place. If desired for added security, using a short stitch length and medium stitch width, zigzag-stitch around each appliqué using matching thread. Press fabric. Sew one button eye in place on each bird.

5. Center fabric on foam-covered headboard. Use straight pins to hold fabric in place. Carefully turn headboard facedown. Referring to manufacturer's instructions, tack or staple fabric to back of headboard. Stand headboard up and remove straight pins.

6. From orange ribbon, cut two 24" lengths and four 3" lengths. From yellow ribbon, cut three 24" lengths and six 3" lengths. For legs, fold each long ribbon length in half, and pin one folded ribbon to bottom center of each bird. To form knees, referring to photo, tie a knot in each ribbon streamer. Pin knees in place. For each foot, tie one short length of matching ribbon around each streamer. Adjust length of legs and trim as needed. Pin feet in place. Using hot-glue gun, glue ribbon to headboard at base of body, at knees, and at feet. Remove all pins.

7. From remaining orange ribbon, cut two 2" lengths. From remaining yellow ribbon, cut three 2" lengths. Tie a knot in center of one orange and one yellow ribbon length. Fold remaining lengths in half, and hot-glue together at fold to hold in place. Referring to photo, hot-glue one ribbon length on top of each bird's head. Trim as necessary.

8. Using permanent marker and referring to dotted lines on pattern, draw mouth, wing, and feathers at top of beak on each bird.

9. Place headboard facedown and attach legs, following manufacturer's instructions.

other ideas

There are lots of items on which these birds can strut their stuff. Fuse one to the front of a throw pillow for an accent for the bed, a chair, or a window seat. Fuse one to a piece of mat board, frame it, and you have an inexpensive piece of artwork.

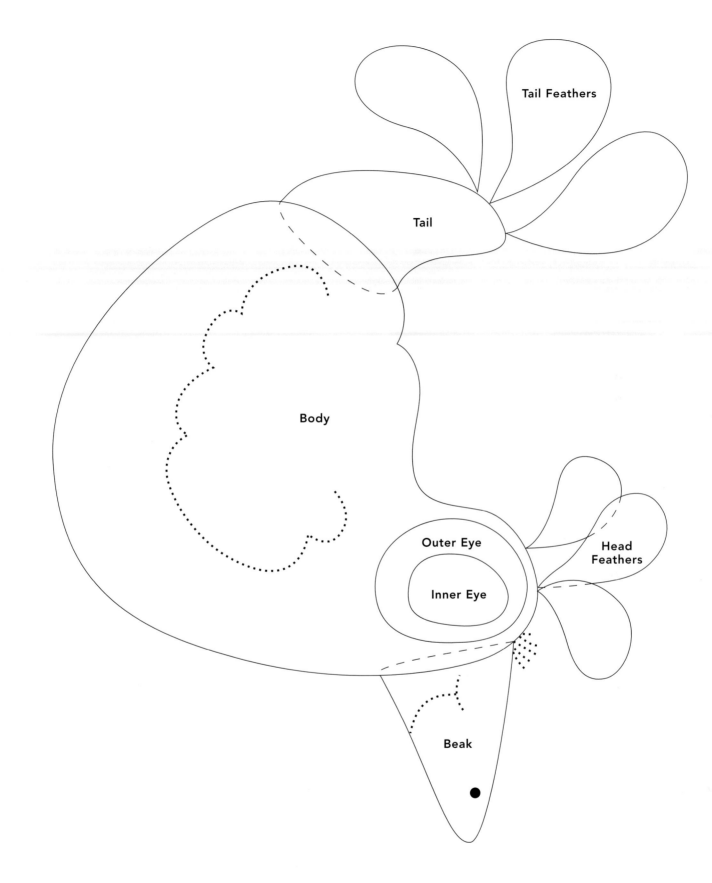

Light dashes indicate lines of underlying pattern pieces.
Bold dashes indicate drawn lines.

All-American Cafe Curtains

Create these charming window treatments with less work than it takes to bake an apple pie! Thanks to Pellon® Wonder-Under®, you can add a touch of Americana to your home without sewing a stitch!

materials

Spring tension curtain rod

Fabric: blue stripe for curtains, blue plaid for trim and ties, red print for stars

¾"-wide Pellon® Wonder-Under® fusible tape

Pellon® Wonder-Under®

Button for each star appliqué

Fabric glue

Spring-type clothespins

Instructions

1. Mount curtain rod over window.
2. To determine width of each curtain panel, measure length of rod; multiply by 1¼. To determine length of each curtain panel, measure from top of curtain rod to desired length; subtract 2½".
3. From blue stripe fabric, cut two panels the determined

measurements. (If necessary, piece fabric by fusing one half-width to each side of one full width. To do this, referring to Appliqué-tions on page 10, press fusible tape onto wrong side of one edge of one half-width. Do not remove paper backing. Turn edge under and press to wrong side. Unfold edge and remove paper backing. Refold edge and fuse in place. Press fusible tape onto right side of one edge of full width. With right sides faceup, place hemmed edge of half-width over taped edge of full width. Fuse fabric widths together. Repeat to fuse remaining half-width to other edge of full width.

4. For fabric trim along bottom of curtains, cut two 13"-wide fabric strips from blue plaid equal in length to width of one curtain panel. Press fusible tape to right side of one curtain panel along bottom edge; remove paper backing. With right sides facing, align one long edge of one trim strip with bottom taped edge of curtain panel. Fuse trim to curtain panel. Fold trim down and press seam allowance toward trim. Repeat for remaining curtain panel.

5. To hem sides of each curtain panel, press fusible tape onto wrong side of each side. Do not remove paper backing. Turn each edge under and press to wrong side. Unfold each edge and remove paper backing. Refold each edge and fuse in place.

6. To hem bottom of curtains, cut two 6" lengths of fusible tape for each panel. Referring to Diagram, press fusible tape onto wrong side of each side edge of curtain trim. For each curtain, cut length of

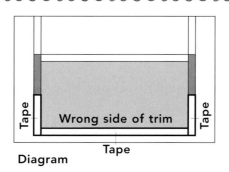

Diagram

fusible tape equal to width of one curtain panel. Press tape onto wrong side of bottom edge of each curtain trim. Do not remove paper backing. Turn lower edge of each curtain trim under 6" and press to wrong side. Unfold and remove paper backing. Refold and fuse in place.

7. To hem top edge of each panel, turn 3" under, pressing to wrong side. Cut two lengths of fusible tape equal in length to one curtain panel width. Press one fusible tape length along top of each 3" pressed edge. Do not remove paper backing. Turn each pressed edge under 3" again and press. Unfold and remove paper backing. Refold and fuse in place.

8. For star appliqués, trace desired number of stars onto paper side of Wonder-Under. Leaving approximately ½" margin, cut around shapes. Press Wonder-Under shapes onto wrong side of red print fabric. Cut out fabric shapes along pattern lines. Remove paper backing. Referring to photo, fuse stars along trim on panels. Glue one button to center of each star. Let dry.

9. To determine number of tab ties for each curtain panel, measure width of one panel and divide by six; round up to next whole number. From blue plaid, cut determined number of 3⅝" x 36" fabric strips. Cut equal number of 36"-long fusible tape lengths.

10. To make ties, press one fusible tape length onto wrong side of one long edge of each blue plaid strip. Do not remove paper backing. Press remaining long edge of each strip to wrong side to meet closest edge of fusible tape. Fold over taped edge along inner edge of tape and press. Unfold and remove paper backing. Refold taped edge and fuse in place.

11. Fold each tie in half, aligning cut ends. For each tie, place a dot of glue between layers 3½" from fold. Secure with clothespins until glue is dry.

12. Spacing ties evenly, position tab ties along top edge of curtain panels with fold of each tie over-lapping 3½" onto right side of panel. Glue overlapped area of each tie to curtain panels. Secure ties with clothespins until glue is dry.

13. To hang curtains, tie tabs in bows around curtain rod.

STAR

page 60

page 54

page 48

Wearable Wonders

Customize a ready-made wardrobe with the stylish appliqués in this chapter. In just a few simple steps, we'll show you how to transform a nondescript garment into a fabulous fashion statement.

48

Spring Blossoms Dress

You're bound to have a zippity-do-dah day when you don this bonny dress. With flowers and ribbons swirling across the front and bees buzzing about, just putting it on makes you feel as though spring is in the air!

materials

¼ yard dark green fabric for ribbon and leaves

¼ yard light green fabric for ribbon, leaves, and stems

Fabric scraps for flowers, bird, and insects

1 yard Pellon® Wonder-Under®

Purchased button-front dress

Black permanent fabric marker

Small needle and white thread

Pastel seed beads

Instructions

1. Wash and dry fabrics. Do not use fabric softener in washer or dryer. Press fabrics.

2. Referring to Appliqué-tions on page 10, press Wonder-Under onto wrong side of fabrics. Referring to photo and ribbon patterns for colors, trace one bird, three bees, three tulips, seven small flowers, one large flower, five small leaves, four medium leaves, three large leaves, one ladybug, and one of each ribbon piece, onto paper side of Wonder-Under. Cut out each shape along pattern lines. Cut three ¼" x 6½" strips from light green fabric for tulip stems. Remove paper backing.

3. Referring to photo for placement, fuse ribbon pieces to front of dress in order indicated on pattern pieces. Fuse bees to collar and front of dress in order indicated on pattern pieces. Fuse two small leaves and two small flowers in place on collar, overlapping as desired. Fuse three small leaves and three small flowers in place on top of Dark Green Ribbon 1, overlapping as desired. Fuse tulip stems in place on top of Dark Green Ribbon 5. Fuse three tulips, two small flowers, one large flower, four medium leaves, and three large leaves in place on top of tulip stems, overlapping as desired. Fuse ladybug in place on top of Light Green Ribbon 6. Fuse bird in place between Light Green Ribbon 2 and Dark Green Ribbon 3.

4. Referring to photo and using black fabric marker, add details and pen stitching lines to appliqués.

5. Sew seed beads to centers of large and small flowers.

other ideas

You'll put "spring" in your step when you fuse several of these appliqués to a pair of canvas espadrilles. Complete your sunny ensemble by adding appliqués to a solid-color fabric purse.

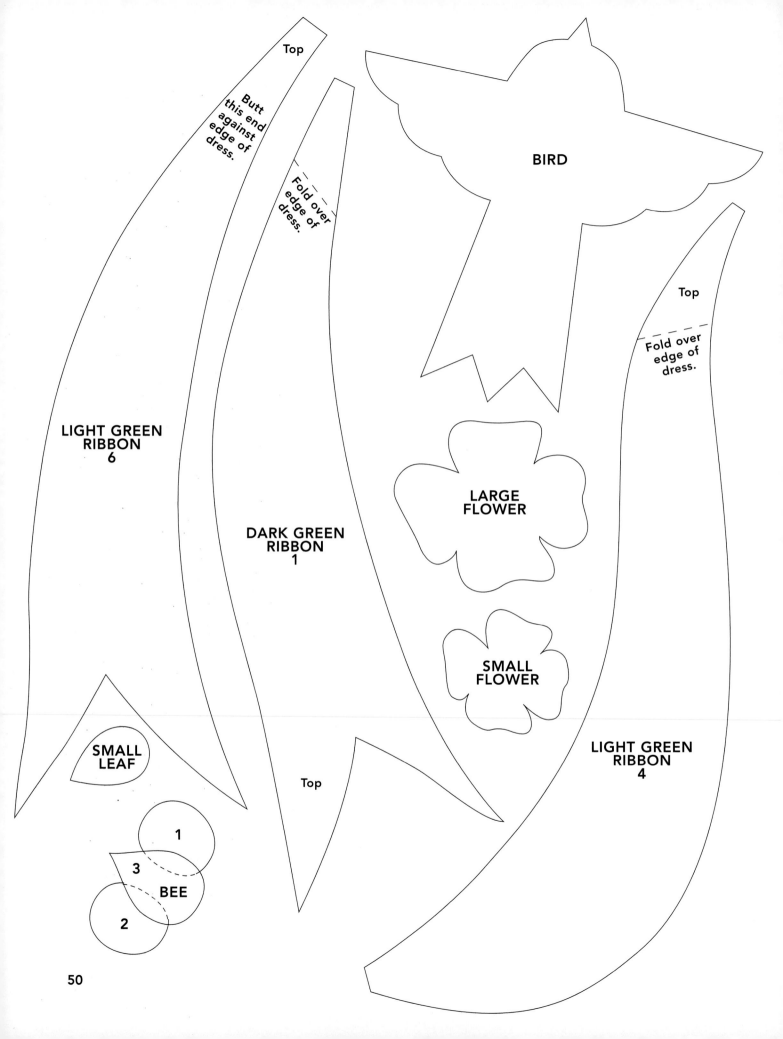

Top

Butt this end against edge of dress.

Fold over edge of dress.

BIRD

Top

Fold over edge of dress.

LIGHT GREEN RIBBON 6

DARK GREEN RIBBON 1

LARGE FLOWER

SMALL FLOWER

SMALL LEAF

Top

LIGHT GREEN RIBBON 4

1

3

BEE

2

50

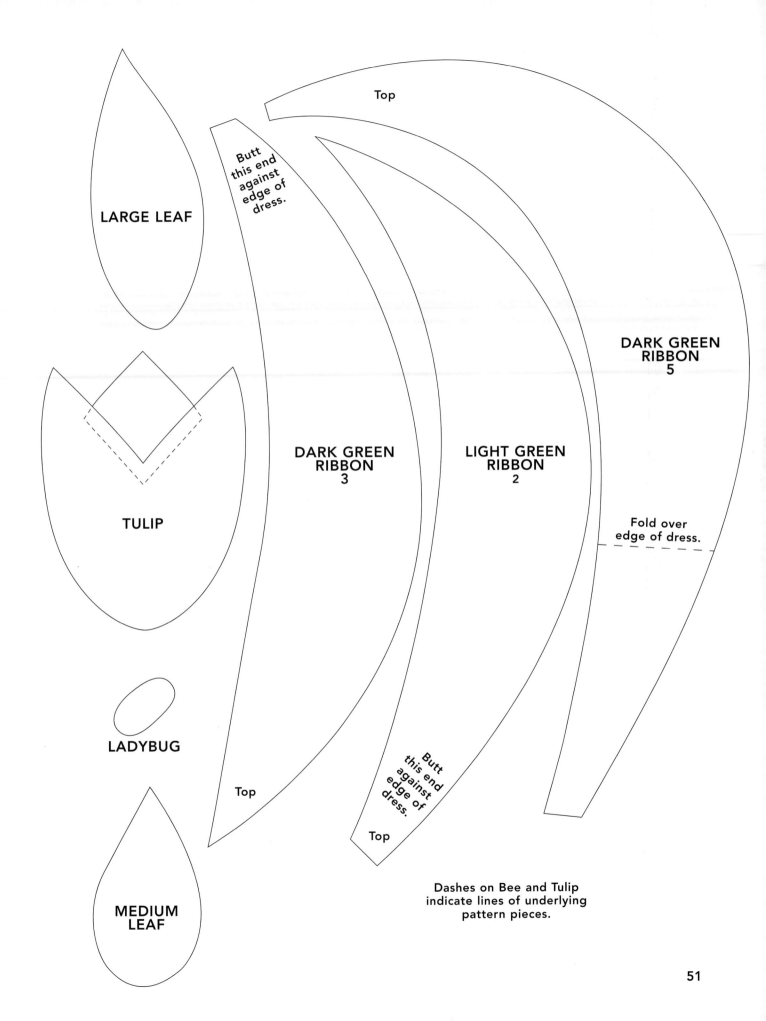

LARGE LEAF

Butt this end against edge of dress.

Top

DARK GREEN RIBBON 5

TULIP

DARK GREEN RIBBON 3

LIGHT GREEN RIBBON 2

Fold over edge of dress.

LADYBUG

Top

Butt this end against edge of dress.

Top

MEDIUM LEAF

Dashes on Bee and Tulip indicate lines of underlying pattern pieces.

Dazzling Dragonfly Vest

Transform a plain, ready-made vest with jewel-toned insects darting here and there. Metallic thread creates the machine-stitched flight path and topstitching on each dragonfly.

materials

⅓ yard Pellon® Wonder-Under®

Jewel-toned fabric scraps

Purchased vest

Metallic sewing thread

Instructions

1. Trace two large dragonflies and four small dragonflies onto paper side of Wonder-Under. Leaving approximately ½" margin, cut around each shape.

2. Referring to Appliqué-tions on page 10, press Wonder-Under shapes onto wrong side of fabric scraps. Cut out fabric shapes along pattern lines.

3. Remove paper backing from each piece.

4. Referring to photo, position pieces of one large dragonfly on left front of vest and fuse in place. Fuse two small dragonflies on right front of vest. Fuse remaining dragonflies, as desired, on vest back.

5. Referring to photo, use metallic thread to machine-stitch along dragonfly bodies and wings. Stitch antennae and loops of flight onto vest.

other ideas

These insects can flutter onto any fashion item—a dress, a jacket, or a baseball cap. Or make a dragonfly book cover for a biology textbook. If you want larger or smaller insects, use a photocopier to enlarge or reduce the pattern as necessary.

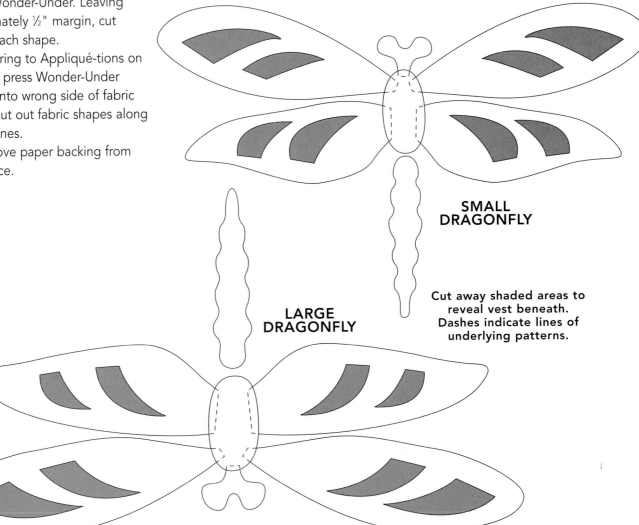

SMALL DRAGONFLY

LARGE DRAGONFLY

Cut away shaded areas to reveal vest beneath. Dashes indicate lines of underlying patterns.

Whimsical Workshirts

Any country girl at heart is bound to love this "egg-stra"-special chick shirt. And for those with stars in their eyes, this heavenly shirt hints of romantic country nights.

materials

For Both

Size 4 or 5 embroidery needle

For Chick Shirt

Purchased long-sleeve, concealed button-front shirt

Assorted yellow and off-white fabric scraps

⅜ yard Pellon® Wonder-Under®

Embroidery floss: colors to coordinate with fabric scraps, brown, orange, green, black

5 (¼"-diameter) black buttons

For Star, Moon, and Heart Shirt

Purchased long-sleeve, button-front shirt

Assorted fabric scraps

½ yard Pellon® Wonder-Under®

Embroidery floss: colors to coordinate with fabric scraps

Buttons in assorted sizes and colors

Instructions for Chick Shirt

Note: Stitch diagrams appear on page 56.

1. Wash and dry shirt; do not use fabric softener in washer or dryer. Hand-wash fabric scraps; iron dry.

2. Referring to Appliqué-tions on page 10, press Wonder-Under onto wrong side of fabric scraps. Trace desired number of motifs onto paper side of Wonder-Under. Cut out shapes along pattern lines. Remove paper backing. Referring to photo, fuse Wonder-Under shapes onto front and arms of shirt.

3. Referring to Diagram A and using three strands of coordinating embroidery floss, blanket-stitch around each chick and egg. Referring to Diagram B and using three strands of brown embroidery floss, make French knots for chicken feed. Referring to Diagram C and patterns, and using three strands of brown embroidery floss, outline-stitch legs and feet. Referring to

Diagram D and patterns, and using three strands of orange embroidery floss, hand satin-stitch beaks. Referring to Diagram E and alternating between three strands of black floss and three strands of green floss, straightstitch grass.

4. Hand-sew one button in place on each chick for eye.

Instructions for Star, Moon, and Heart Shirt

Note: Stitch diagrams appear on page 56.

1. To apply appliqués, repeat steps 1 and 2 for Chick Shirt.

2. Referring to Diagram A and using four strands of coordinating embroidery floss, blanket-stitch around each design. Using six strands of embroidery floss, blanket-stitch around collar and cuffs and along shoulder seams.

3. Referring to photo, use embroidery floss to hand-sew buttons to front placket of shirt and to center of several stars.

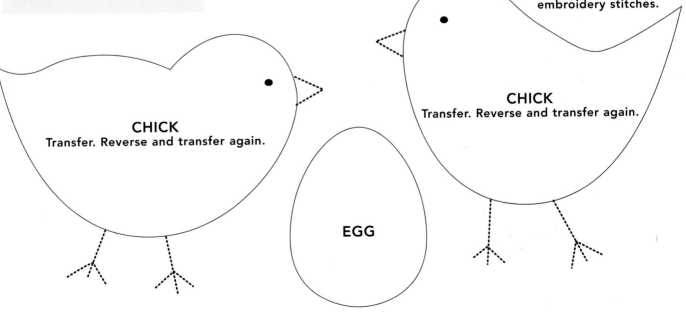

Dashed lines indicate embroidery stitches.

CHICK
Transfer. Reverse and transfer again.

EGG

CHICK
Transfer. Reverse and transfer again.

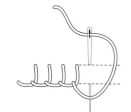

Diagram A
Blanket Stitch

Knot one end of floss. Push needle up from wrong side of garment, even with edge of appliqué. Insert needle into appliqué, then come up at edge again, keeping floss below point of needle. Continue stitching in same manner, keeping stitches even. Stitches should be approximately 3/16" long and 1/4" apart.

Diagram B
French Knot

Knot one end of floss. Push needle up from wrong side of garment. Wrap end of floss closest to garment around needle twice. Reinsert needle into garment next to first stitch, holding end of floss with free hand. Tighten knot; then pull needle through, holding floss until it must be released.

Diagram C
Outline Stitch

Knot one end of floss. Push needle up from wrong side of garment. With thumb holding floss above stitches, insert needle down and up in garment as shown, keeping stitches even.

Diagram D
Satin Stitch

Knot one end of floss. Push needle up from wrong side of garment. Place stitches side-by-side as shown until area is filled.

Diagram E
Straight Stitch

Knot one end of floss. Push needle up from wrong side of garment. Insert needle up and down in garment as shown. Stitch lengths may be varied as desired.

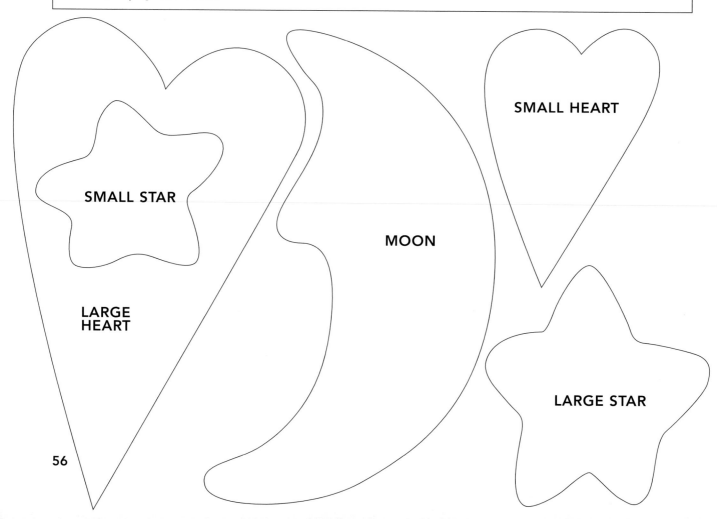

SMALL STAR

SMALL HEART

MOON

LARGE HEART

LARGE STAR

Trick-or-Treat Tops

Wear one of these quick-to-make tops when you're on the prowl for Halloween treats. They are also ideal for wearing to a pumpkin party or when escorting your children as they trick-or-treat. You'll be thrilled these black cats crossed your path!

materials

For Both

Purchased sweatshirt with set-in sleeves

Clear nylon sewing thread

For Cardigan

Fabric: ¾ yard 45"-wide black-and-white stripe for binding, 15" x 8" piece orange-and-yellow check for square appliqués, 6" x 10" piece black for cat appliqués, scraps for star appliqués

2 yards Pellon® Wonder-Under®

Rotary cutter with pinking blade

White embroidery floss

Embroidery needle

10 (¾") black buttons

6 assorted buttons

For Sweatshirt

Fabric: ½ yard 45"-wide orange-and-yellow check, ⅛ yard 45"-wide black-and-white stripe, 12" square black for cat appliqués

1 yard Pellon® Wonder-Under®

4 (½") star-shaped buttons

Instructions for Cardigan

1. Wash and dry sweatshirt; do not use fabric softener in washer or dryer. Hand-wash fabric scraps; iron dry.

2. Remove cuffs, neckband, and bottom band from sweatshirt. Cut sleeves to desired length. Locate center front of sweatshirt by matching shoulder and armhole seams and folding sweatshirt in half lengthwise. Cut along center front fold. (Be sure to cut front of sweatshirt only.)

3. Staystitch neckline edge, lower edge, sleeve edges, and center front edges by straightstitching approximately ½" from cut edges. (When staystitching neckline, stitch from shoulder seams toward center front and center back.)

4. For bias binding, referring to Diagram, fold fabric. Cut along fold. Discard triangular section of fabric. Cut a 10" x 25" piece of Wonder-Under. Referring to Appliqué-tions on page 10, press Wonder-Under, paper side up, onto wrong side of binding fabric with one long edge along bias edge of fabric.

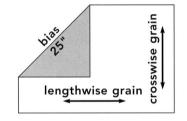

Diagram

5. To bind neckline, measure neckline edge. Use rotary cutter with pinking blade to cut a 1¼"-wide bias strip from binding fabric, same length as determined measurement. Do not remove paper backing. With wrong sides facing and raw edges aligned, press bias strip in half lengthwise. Unfold binding and remove paper backing. Insert neckline edge of cardigan in fold of binding; fuse.

6. Repeat Step 5 to bind lower edge and center front edges.

7. For sleeve bindings, measure raw edge of one sleeve; add 1". Use rotary cutter and pinking blade to cut two 1¼"-wide bias strips from binding fabric, same length as determined measurement. Do not remove paper backing. With wrong sides facing and raw edges aligned, press bias strips in half lengthwise. Unfold each binding and remove paper backing. Beginning at sleeve seam, insert one sleeve edge in fold of one binding; fuse, overlapping ends. Repeat for other sleeve.

8. Using six strands of embroidery floss and referring to photo and Diagram B on page 64, work running stitch along bound edges.

9. Press Wonder-Under pieces onto wrong side of appliqué fabrics. Draw two 5¼" squares on paper side of black-and-white fabric (we cut ours on bias), and draw two 4¼" squares on paper side of orange-and-yellow check fabric. Cut out squares along marked lines. Remove paper backing. Trace one cat onto paper side of black fabric. Reverse pattern and trace again. Cut out cats along marked lines. Remove paper backing. Transfer Star Part A and Star Part B patterns four times each onto paper side of fabric scraps. Cut out shapes along marked lines. Remove paper backing.

10. Referring to photo, arrange appliqués on cardigan; fuse. If desired for added security, using clear nylon thread, zigzag over raw edges of appliqués using narrow stitch width and short stitch length.

11. Make pleat on lower edge of each sleeve. Sew one ¾" button through all layers of each pleat.

12. Hand-sew one ¾" button to each corner of square appliqués. Hand-sew assorted buttons randomly on front of cardigan.

Instructions for Sweatshirt

1. Wash and dry sweatshirt; do not use fabric softener in washer or dryer. Hand-wash fabric scraps; iron dry.

2. Measure front of sweatshirt from armhole to armhole 2½" below neckband; add 6". Cut one 5¼"-wide strip from orange-and-yellow check fabric and two 1"-wide strips from black-and-white stripe fabric equal in length to determined measurement.

3. With right sides facing, raw edges aligned, and using ¼" seam allowance, stitch one 1"-wide strip to 5¼"-wide strip along one long edge. Press seam toward orange-and-yellow check fabric. Fold raw edge of black-and-white stripe fabric under ¼"; press to wrong side. Repeat to stitch remaining 1"-wide strip to remaining side of 5¼"-wide strip.

4. Cut piece of Wonder-Under 6" less than length of stitched strip and ½" less than width of stitched strip. Referring to Appliqué-tions on page 10, center and press Wonder-Under strip onto wrong side of stitched strip. Remove paper backing.

5. Center stitched strip across front of sweatshirt so that top long edge is 2½" below neckband. Using seam ripper, open armhole seams as far as necessary to insert ends of strip into sweatshirt at seams. Fuse strip in place.

6. Topstitch along seams and pressed edges of strip. Trim short edges of strip even with raw edges of armholes. Turn sweatshirt wrong side out, and stitch armhole seams closed along previous seam lines.

7. Trace cat pattern onto paper side of Wonder-Under twice. Reverse pattern and trace twice more. Leaving approximately ½" margin, cut out around shapes. Press Wonder-Under shapes onto wrong side of black fabric. Cut out

fabric shapes along marked lines. Remove paper backing.

8. Referring to photo for placement, fuse cat appliqués to strip on sweatshirt. If desired for added security, using clear nylon thread, zigzag over raw edges of appliqués using narrow stitch width and short stitch length.

9. Referring to photo, hand-sew one star button to center of each appliqué.

other ideas

When setting about the serious business of treat collecting, little goblins need a sturdy bag that will hold up under the weight of all that candy. For a festive solution, purchase a plain canvas tote bag, and embellish it with fused black cat appliqués.

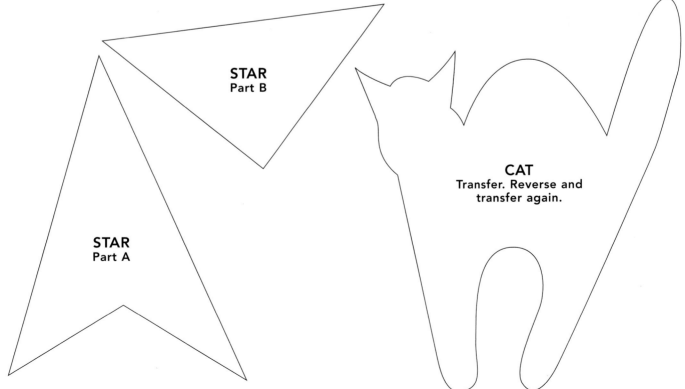

STAR
Part B

STAR
Part A

CAT
Transfer. Reverse and transfer again.

Patriotic Patch Tees

Show off your patriotic side with tops as hot as a firecracker and as bright as a star. If you choose, embellish the motifs with free-motion quilting. Or for a quick-and-easy alternative, highlight them with fabric paint. With Pellon® Wonder-Under®, no sewing is required.

materials

For Both

Spray starch

Disappearing-ink fabric marker

¼ yard Pellon® Wonder-Under®

Blue rayon thread

For Firecracker Shirt

Fabric: ¼ yard royal blue solid, ¼ yard red-and-white stripe, red-and-white print scraps

White rayon thread

Purchased red T-shirt

For Star Shirt

Fabric: ½ yard red-and-white stripe, ¼ yard white, 3 (5") squares blue print

Red rayon thread

Purchased blue T-shirt

Instructions for Firecracker Shirt

1. From blue solid fabric, cut two 9" x 13" panels. From red-and-white stripe fabric, cut one 9" x 13" panel. Heavily spray starch on wrong side of each panel; iron dry.
2. With right sides up, sandwich stripe panel between blue panels. Using fabric marker, draw 6" x 10" rectangle at center of top panel.

With blue thread, stitch along marked line, stitching through all layers.
3. Referring to Appliqué-tions on page 10, press Wonder-Under to wrong side of red-and-white scraps. Trace five rectangles 1" to 1¼" wide by 3" to 4" long on paper side of red-and-white scraps. Cut out shapes along pattern lines. Referring to photo for position, fuse shapes to panels.
4. Using white thread, stitch each firecracker with free-motion quilting. Staying within stitched rectangle, stitch firecracker fuses.
5. Trim panels ½" outside stitched rectangle. Create fringe by clipping at ½" intervals up to but not through stitching line of each panel.
6. Center firecracker panel on red T-shirt 1" below front neckline seam. Stitch panel to shirt by stitching over stitched rectangle. Machine-wash and dry shirts to fluff fringe.

Instructions for Star Shirt

1. From red-and-white stripe fabric, cut two 9" x 13" panels. From white fabric, cut one 9" x 13" panel. Heavily spray starch on wrong side of each panel; iron dry.
2. Referring to Step 2 of Firecracker Shirt, sandwich white panel

between stripe panels, and stitch panels together. Using red thread, channel-quilt layers together by stitching along every few red stripes.
3. Referring to Appliqué-tions on page 10, press Wonder-Under to wrong side of 5" blue print squares. Trace one large star and two small stars onto paper side of blue squares. Cut out shapes along pattern lines. Referring to photo for position, fuse shapes to panels.
4. Using blue thread, stitch each star with free-motion quilting. Refer to steps 5–6 of Firecracker Shirt to create fringe and to stitch panel to front of blue T-shirt.

other ideas

Your whole family can celebrate our nation's independence in style, thanks to these spirited appliqués. Make a shirt for yourself, then apply firecracker or star appliqués to a pair of children's overalls. Add flag-waving flair to your table by fusing these motifs to the hem of a red, white, or blue tablecloth.

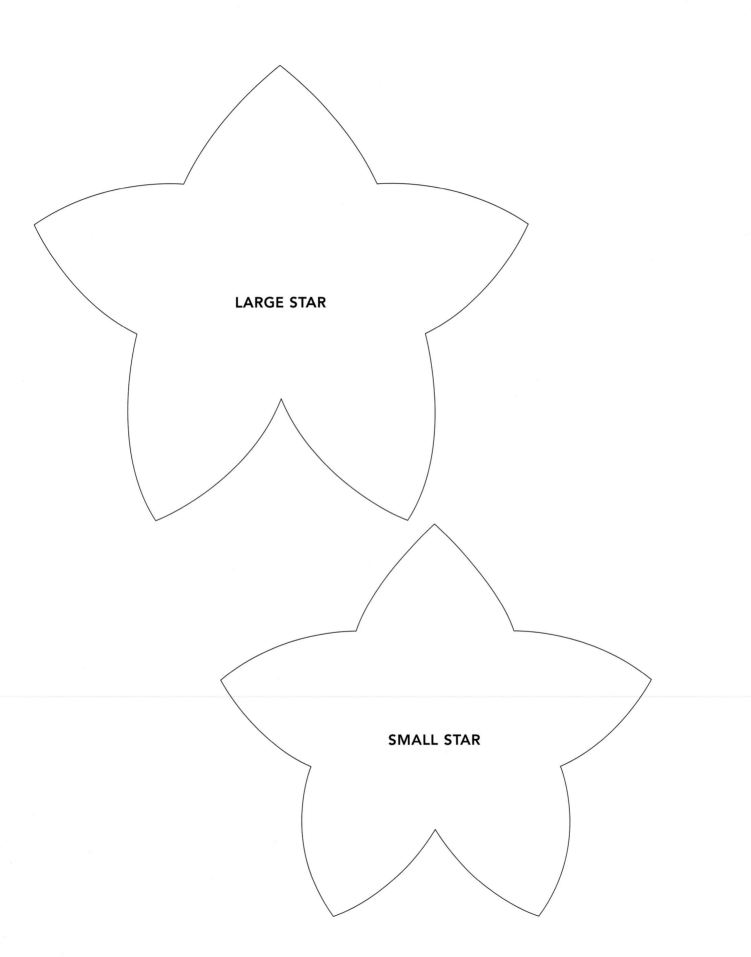

LARGE STAR

SMALL STAR

May Day Cardigan

Take the opportunity on May 1 to show your best friend or mother how much
she means to you by presenting her with this flower-covered jacket. Made from a
sweatshirt, this lightweight cardigan is just right for cool spring days.

materials

Purchased sweatshirt with set-in sleeves

Assorted fabric scraps

Flower-printed fabric scraps (flower motifs should measure approximately 2" in diameter)

¾ yard 45"-wide fabric for binding

2 yards Pellon® Wonder-Under®

Rotary cutter with pinking blade

Coordinating embroidery floss

Embroidery needle

Buttons: 5 assorted for flower centers, 2 (¾") for sleeves

Instructions

1. Wash and dry sweatshirt; do not use fabric softener in washer or dryer. Hand-wash fabric scraps; iron dry.

2. Remove cuffs, neckband, and bottom band from sweatshirt. Cut sleeves to desired length. Locate center front of sweatshirt by matching shoulder and armhole seams and folding sweatshirt in half lengthwise. Cut along center front fold. (Be sure to cut front of sweatshirt only.)

3. Staystitch neckline edge, lower edge, sleeve edges, and center front edges by straightstitching approximately ¾" from cut edges. (When staystitching neckline, stitch from shoulder seams toward center front and center back.)

4. For bias binding, referring to Diagram A, fold fabric. Cut along fold. Discard triangular section of fabric. Cut a 10" x 25" piece of Wonder-Under. Referring to Appliqué-tions on page 10, press Wonder-Under, paper side up, onto wrong side of binding fabric with one long edge along bias edge of fabric.

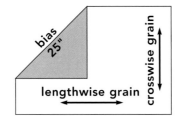

Diagram A

5. To bind neckline, measure raw edge of neckline. Use rotary cutter with pinking blade to cut a 1¼"-wide bias strip from binding fabric, same length as determined measurement. Do not remove paper backing. With wrong sides facing and raw edges aligned, press bias strip in half lengthwise. Unfold binding and remove paper backing. Insert neckline edge of sweatshirt in fold of binding; fuse.

6. Repeat Step 5 to bind lower edge and center front edges of cardigan, cutting as many bias strips as necessary.

7. For sleeve bindings, measure raw edge of one sleeve; add 1". Use rotary cutter with pinking blade to cut two 1¼"-wide bias strips from binding fabric, same length as determined measurement. Do not remove paper backing. With wrong sides facing and raw edges aligned, press bias strips in half lengthwise. Unfold each binding and remove paper backing. Beginning at sleeve seam, insert one sleeve edge in fold of one binding; fuse, overlapping ends. Repeat for other sleeve.

8. Using six strands of embroidery floss and referring to photo and Diagram B, work running stitch along bound edges.

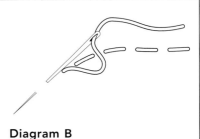

**Diagram B
Running Stitch**
Knot one end of floss. Bring needle up from wrong side of garment. Insert needle back down into garment, then come up from wrong side one stitch space away. Continue stitching in same manner.

9. For printed flowers, select designs from printed fabric. Cut pieces of Wonder-Under slightly larger than designs. Press Wonder-Under pieces onto wrong side of fabric under selected designs. Cut out desired number of flowers. Remove paper backing.

10. Trace four leaves, five double leaves, five flowers, five flower centers, one handle, one basket, and one stripe onto paper side of Wonder-Under. Leaving approximately ½" margin, cut around each shape. Press Wonder-Under shapes onto wrong side of fabric scraps. Cut out fabric shapes along pattern lines. Remove paper backing. Referring to photo, fuse fabric shapes to front of cardigan.

11. Using three strands of embroidery floss and referring to Diagram A on page 56, blanket-stitch around round flowers and all leaves. If desired for added security, using clear nylon thread, zigzag over raw edges of basket, handle, stripe, and printed flowers using narrow stitch width and short stitch length.

12. Sew buttons to centers of round flowers. Make small pleat on lower edge of each sleeve. Secure pleat by sewing one ¾" button through all layers of each pleat.

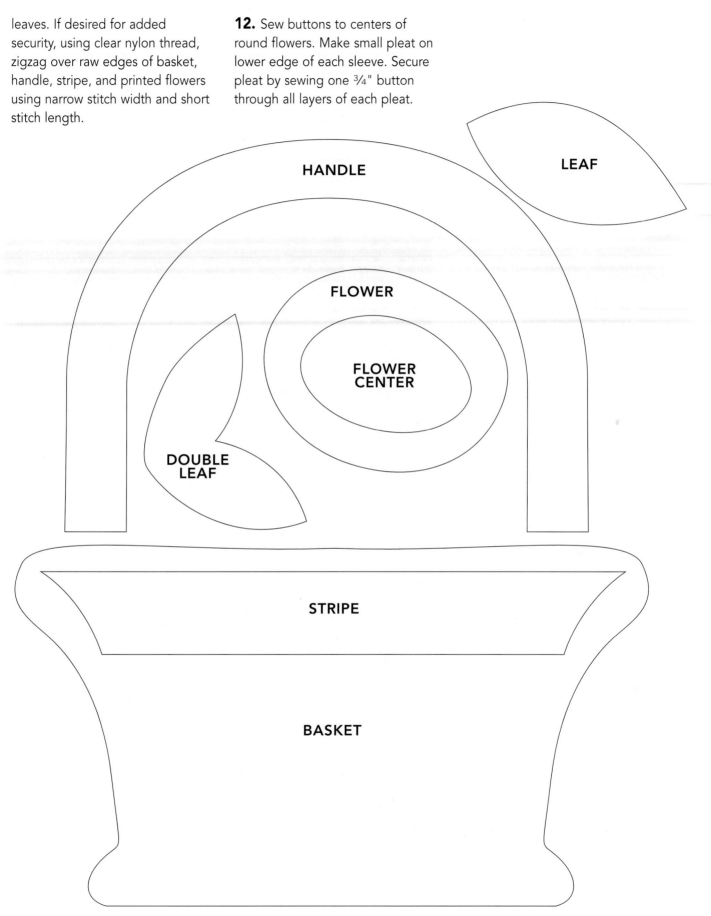

HANDLE

LEAF

FLOWER

FLOWER CENTER

DOUBLE LEAF

STRIPE

BASKET

Folk Art Blazer

These appliqués are as inviting as the cozy wool blazer they adorn. A thrift store is a great source for an inexpensive blazer. If you find one you love, but it has begun to show a bit of wear, give it a fresh new look by simply patching any thin spots with appliqués.

materials

Fusible interfacing scraps

Assorted fabric scraps for appliqués

Pellon® Wonder-Under® scraps

Purchased wool blazer

Coordinating embroidery floss

Embroidery needle

Instructions

1. Press interfacing onto wrong side of fabric scraps.

2. Trace desired number of each shape onto paper side of Wonder-Under. Leaving approximately ½" margin, cut around each shape. Referring to Appliqué-tions on page 10, press Wonder-Under shapes onto wrong side of inter-faced fabric scraps. Cut out fabric shapes along pattern lines. Remove paper backings.

3. Fuse fabric shapes as desired to front of blazer.

4. Referring to photo and Diagram A on page 56, use three strands of embroidery floss to work blanket stitches along edges of appliqués and along edges of blazer.

Referring to photo and Diagram A on page 56

other ideas

These homespun appliqué motifs are charming whether accenting a blazer or adorning the branches of a Christmas tree. To make folk art ornaments, simply fuse two pieces of fabric together with Wonder-Under, then transfer the desired shape and cut out the ornament. If desired, work blanket stitches along the edges of each ornament.

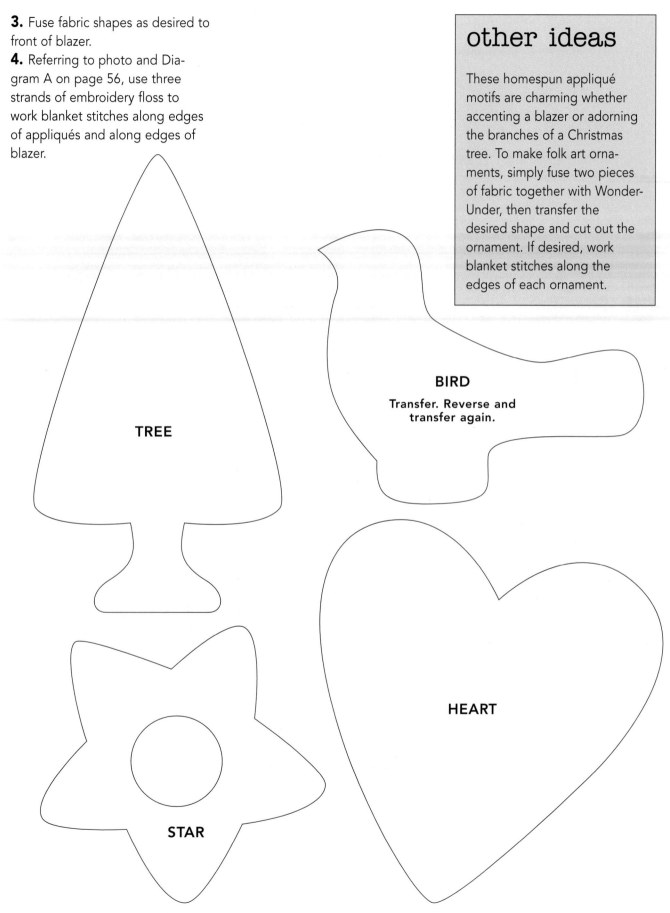

TREE

BIRD

Transfer. Reverse and transfer again.

HEART

STAR

Study in Suede

Create a jacket that looks like a designer original with this elegant leaf appliqué. The curving lines and warm golden color of this faux suede leaf design is a striking contrast to the straight lines and black background of the jacket. The end result is haute couture.

materials

½ yard Pellon® Wonder-Under®

¼ yard Ultrasuede®

Purchased jacket without lapels

Water-soluble stabilizer

Lightweight clear nylon thread

Thread to match jacket lining

Instructions

1. Trace three leaf designs onto paper side of Wonder-Under. Reverse pattern and trace three more leaf designs. Leaving approximately ½" margin, cut around each shape. Referring to Appliqué-tions on page 10, press Wonder-Under shapes onto wrong side of Ultrasuede. Cut out fabric shapes along pattern lines. Remove paper backing.

2. Referring to photo, position leaf designs on front of jacket to determine desired placement. (Stem on one leaf will lap under Leaf A.) Trim stems if necessary so that only ⅛" of stem extends under Leaf A. Using damp fabric press cloth and lots of steam, fuse leaf designs in place by lightly gliding iron over shapes.

3. Pin stabilizer to lining to provide extra support when satin-stitching edges of leaves. Using nylon thread in top of machine and matching thread in bobbin, satin-stitch edges of leaves using very small zigzag stitch. Remove excess stabilizer.

other ideas

Rather than overlapping this leaf design to create one long motif, consider shortening the stem and placing the design randomly across the front of the jacket.

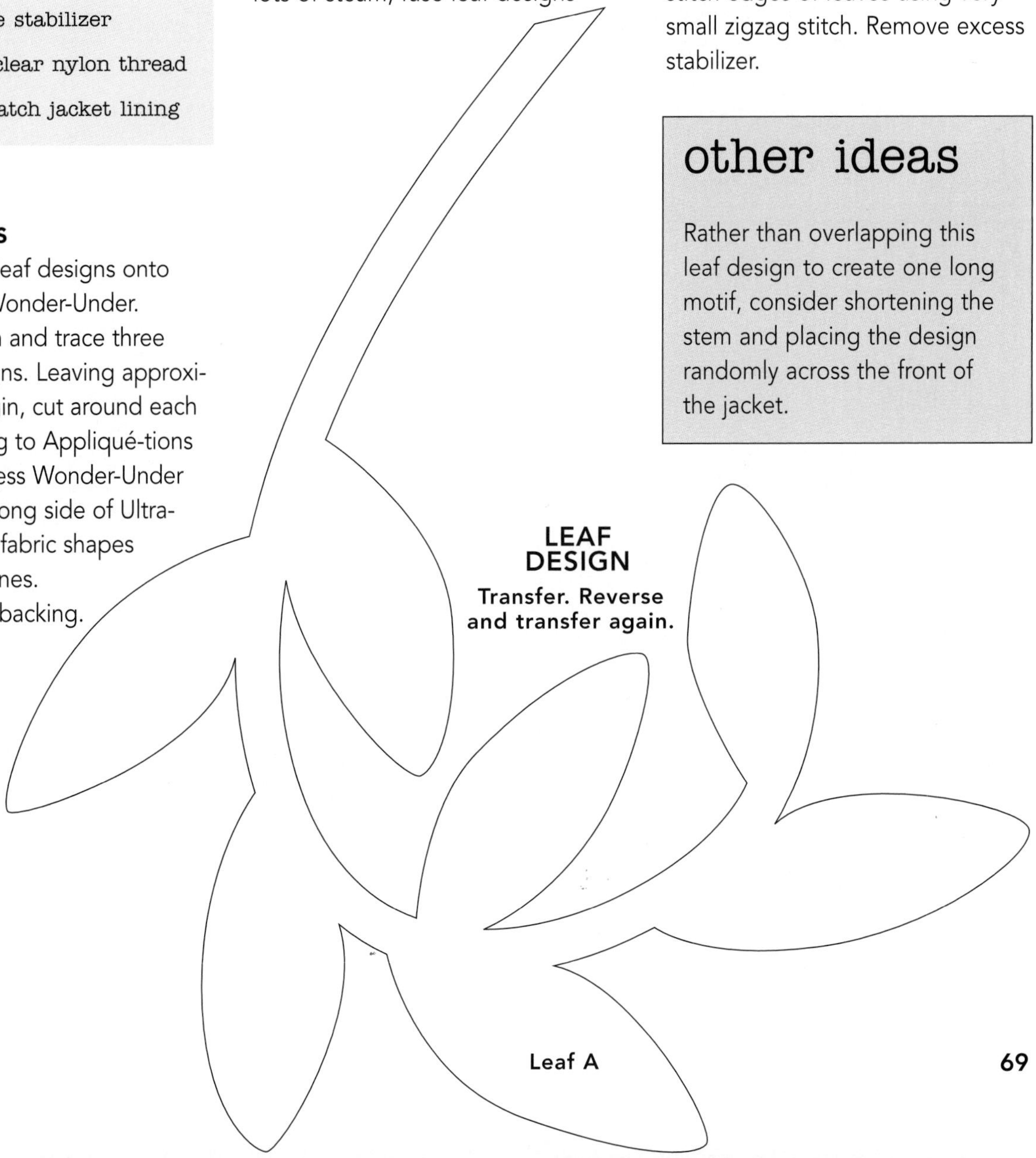

LEAF DESIGN

Transfer. Reverse and transfer again.

Leaf A

Snowman Sweatshirt

Designed by Kim Eidson Crane

Make a favorite sweatshirt even cooler with a few frosty appliqués.
Decorative embroidery and machine stitches add folksy appeal.

materials

¼ yard Pellon® Wonder-Under®

Plaid flannel scrap

Muslin scraps

Purchased navy sweatshirt

Gray blue thread

¼" shank buttons: 2 black,
1 red

3 (⅜") black flat buttons

Ecru embroidery floss

8" length ⅞"-wide red ribbon

Small safety pin

Instructions

1. Trace snowman hat onto paper side of Wonder-Under. Leaving approximately ½" margin, cut around hat shape. Referring to Appliqué-tions on page 10, press Wonder-Under hat shape onto wrong side of flannel scrap. Cut out hat along pattern lines. Remove paper backing.

2. Trace snowman body, head, and arm patterns onto paper side of Wonder-Under. Reverse arm pattern and trace again. Cut out snowman shapes along pattern lines. Press shapes onto wrong side of muslin scraps, leaving 1" between each piece. Leaving approximately ¼" margin, cut out snowman pieces. Remove paper backing. (Edges of muslin pieces will begin to fray, adding homespun appeal to appliqué design.)

3. Referring to photo for placement, center snowman body on sweatshirt front. Fuse body in place. Using gray blue thread and medium-width zigzag, stitch

around edges of body, keeping all zigzag stitches on muslin. Fuse snowman head and arms in place. Zigzag-stitch as for body. Fuse snowman hat in place. Zigzag-stitch as for body.

4. Referring to photo, sew two black shank buttons to face for eyes. Sew red shank button to face for nose. Sew black flat buttons down front of body.

5. Using six strands of embroidery floss and referring to Diagram B on page 56, make row of French knots for snowman mouth. Using 12 strands of floss, make French knot snowflakes on sweatshirt around snowman appliqué.

6. To make scarf, fray ends of red ribbon. Tie knot at ribbon center. Attach scarf to neck of snowman with safety pin. Remove scarf before laundering.

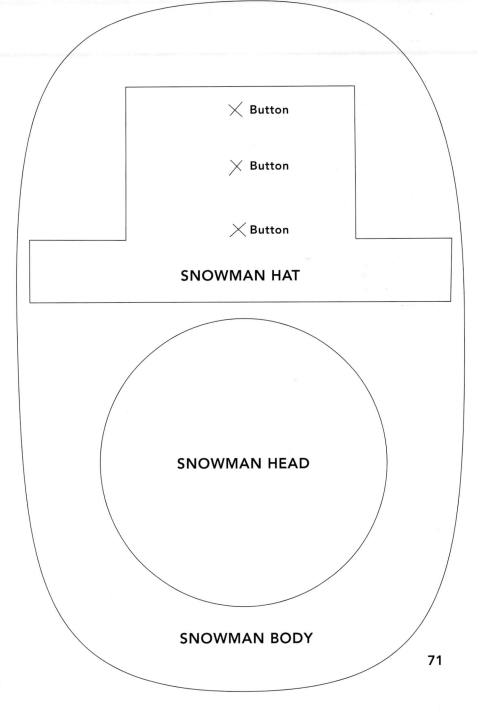

✕ **Button**

✕ **Button**

✕ **Button**

SNOWMAN HAT

SNOWMAN HEAD

SNOWMAN BODY

SNOWMAN ARM

Transfer. Reverse and transfer again.

page 101

page 74

page 84

Childhood Wonders

The imagery and fun of childhood is captured in the playful patterns featured in this chapter. From dolls to dresses, from bumper pads to belly bags, these projects are quick to make because fusible web eliminates much of the time-consuming detail work.

Sweet Dreams

Your newborn will drift off into peaceful slumber when surrounded by these motifs inspired by the nighttime sky. A thin wisp of organdy covers the appliqués and adds a dreamlike quality to the designs.

materials

½ yard Pellon® Wonder-Under®

Fabric: ¼ yard yellow, ¼ yard white, 2⅓ yards bright blue, ⅔ yard blue-and-white stripe

Black permanent fabric marker

1½ yards white polyester organdy

15 yards ⅝"-wide yellow grosgrain ribbon

Batting

Yellow pearl cotton

Darning needle

Instructions

Note: Seam allowances are ½".

1. Trace 12 moons, 12 large stars, and 12 small stars onto paper side of Wonder-Under. Leaving approximately ½" margin, cut around each shape. Referring to Appliqué-tions on page 10, press Wonder-Under moon shapes onto wrong side of yellow fabric. Press Wonder-Under star shapes onto wrong side of white fabric. Cut out fabric shapes along pattern lines. Remove paper backing. Set appliqués aside.

2. For side bumpers, from bright blue fabric, cut four 54½" x 8¼" lengths. Fold two lengths into quarters. Unfold and mark fold lines with pins. Referring to photo for placement, center one moon, one large star, and one small star in each quarter section. Fuse appliqués in place.

3. For end bumpers, from bright blue fabric, cut four 30" x 8¼" lengths. Fold two lengths in half widthwise. Unfold and mark fold line with pins. Referring to photo for placement, center one moon, one large star, and one small star in each half section. Fuse appliqués in place.

4. Using fabric marker and referring to pattern, draw eye and mouth on each moon. From organdy, cut two 54½" x 8¼" lengths and two 30" x 8¼" lengths. Lay corresponding organdy lengths over appliquéd lengths and baste together.

5. For trim, from blue-and-white stripe fabric, cut two 54½" x 4½"

strips, piecing as needed to obtain length; and two 30" x 4½" strips. With right sides facing and raw edges aligned, stitch one corresponding blue-and-white strip to top edge of each appliquéd bumper length. Set aside.

6. To make side bumper backs, fold remaining side bumper lengths in quarters. Unfold and mark fold lines with pins. Cut 22 (24") lengths from ribbon. Fold 14 lengths of ribbon in half. Referring to Diagram, stitch three folded ribbon lengths to top edge of each side bumper length, positioning ribbons at marked fold lines. Stitch two folded ribbon lengths to each end of side bumper lengths, positioning ribbons ¾" from top and bottom edges.

7. Fold remaining ribbon lengths in half. To make end bumper backs, stitch two folded ribbon lengths to ends of each remaining end bumper length, positioning ribbons ¾" from top and bottom edges.

8. Before joining bumper fronts to bumper backs, pin ribbon lengths on bumper backs to keep ribbons free from stitching. With right sides facing, align top raw edge of bumper backs with raw edge of

blue-and-white stripe trim on corresponding bumper fronts. Stitch across top edge.

9. From batting, cut two 54½" x 10" lengths and two 30" x 10" lengths. With bottom edges aligned, baste corresponding batting length to wrong side of each bumper back. (Batting will extend into trim.) Slide each bumper back down slightly so bottom edge aligns with bottom edge of bumper front. Stitching through all layers, stitch side edges and bottom edge of bumpers, leaving 6"-opening in center of bottom edge for turning. Trim batting and turn bumpers right side out.

10. Match and pin seam lines of striped trim together. Stitch on seam line through all three layers. Turn raw edges of opening under and whipstitch closed.

11. Thread darning needle with doubled length of pearl cotton, but do not knot. To tie bumper layers together, working from back of bumper, push needle up through front and then back down to back. Tie pearl cotton in tight double knot. Leaving short tails, trim pearl cotton. Repeat randomly along bumpers.

12. Tie bumpers to crib.

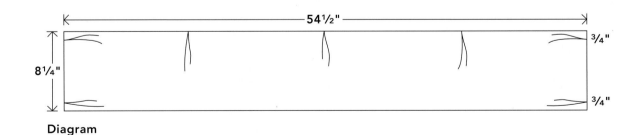

Diagram

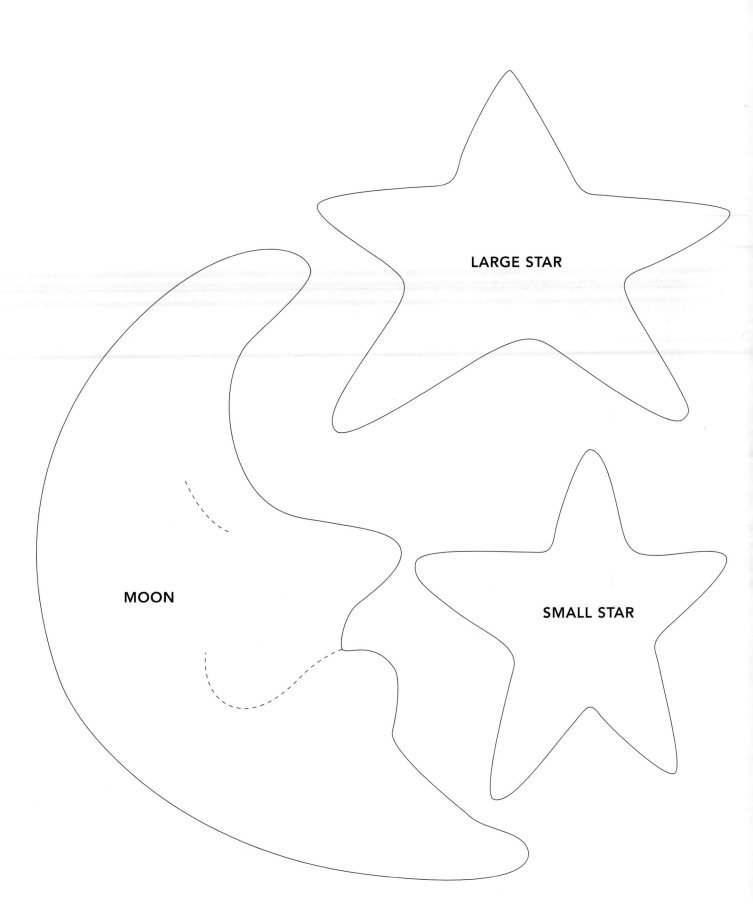

LARGE STAR

MOON

SMALL STAR

Dashed lines are drawn lines.

Cuddly Crib Shirts

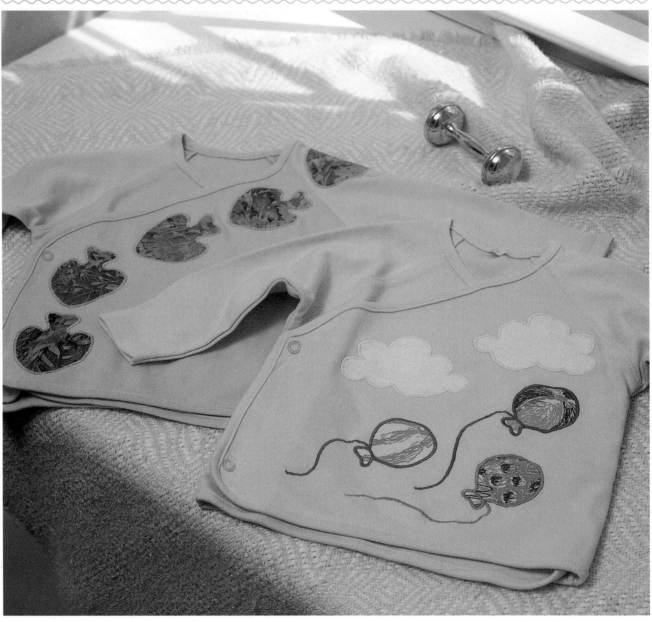

Add a loving touch to a plain purchased baby shirt. Appliqué drifting balloons floating across the front or colorful fish swimming along the edge.

materials

For each

¼ yard Pellon® Wonder-Under®

Purchased kimono baby shirt

½ yard tear-away fabric stabilizer

For fish shirt

⅛ yard fabric for fish

Thread to match fabric

For balloon shirt

⅛ yard fabric for balloons

⅛ yard white fabric for clouds

Disappearing-ink fabric marker

Thread to match fabrics

Instructions

1. Trace desired number and style of appliqué patterns onto paper side of Wonder-Under. Leaving approximately ½" margin, cut around each shape. Referring to Appliqué-tions on page 10, press

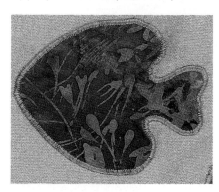

Wonder-Under shapes onto wrong side of corresponding fabrics. Cut out shapes along pattern lines. Remove paper backing.

2. Referring to photo, position appliqués on shirt and fuse in place. For balloons, draw strings with disappearing-ink fabric marker.

3. Pin tear-away stabilizer behind design areas. Using matching thread, satin-stitch designs using medium-width zigzag. For balloon strings, satin-stitch along drawn lines. Gently tear away stabilizer from garment.

other ideas

You can use these appliqués to create a whole layette. For example, apply a cluster of beautiful balloons to the lower edge of a cotton thermal blanket. Or fuse a school of friendly fish to the edge of a hooded bath towel.

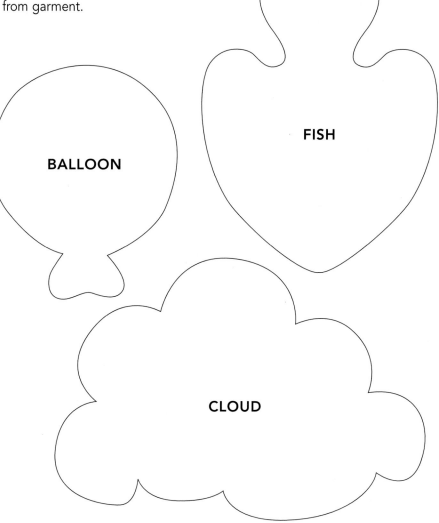

BALLOON

FISH

CLOUD

All-About-Town Play Mat

Designed by Kim Eidson Crane

This oversized play mat is the "driving force" behind hours of creative play.
Whether your son's parking his car or speeding a fire truck to rescue a kitten stuck in a tree,
this portable town is sure to spark his imagination.

materials

1⅔ yards 60"-wide royal blue medium-to-heavyweight fabric

6½ yards green wide bias tape

3 yards Pellon® Wonder-Under®

45"-wide medium-weight fabrics: ⅛ yard each light blue, orange, red, yellow; ⅝ yard green

⅛ yard each vinyl fabric: green, black

Thread: royal blue, green, black, yellow

Puffy fabric paint (optional): royal blue, green, black

Buttons: 8 (½") blue round, 28 (⅝") yellow square

Ribbon: 2 yards ⅛"-wide yellow, 3½ yards ¼"-wide green, 3½ yards 3"-wide yellow

10 yards nylon cording

Instructions

Finished Size: Approximately 60" square

1. Turn cut edges of royal blue fabric under ½"; press. Working from wrong side, zigzag over raw edges, stitching hem in place. From bias tape, cut four 58" lengths. Turn bias tape ends under ¼"; stitch. To make casing, referring to Diagram, on wrong side of blue play mat, center one bias tape length along each edge. If tape overlaps at corners, shorten one or both lengths. Edgestitch long edges of bias tape, leaving short ends open.

2. Referring to Appliqué-tions on page 10, press Wonder-Under onto wrong side of following fabrics: light blue, orange, red, yellow, green vinyl, and black vinyl. Do not remove paper backing.

3. From light blue fabric, cut following: two 4" squares for houses, two 1½" x 2½" rectangles for house doors, one 4" x 8" rectangle and one 4" x 7" rectangle for buildings, and one 1¾" x 4" rectangle and one 1¾" x 2" rectangle for building doors. Trace two rooftops on Wonder-Under side of light blue fabric. Cut out along pattern lines.

4. From orange fabric, cut following: two 4" squares for houses, one 1½" x 2½" rectangle for house door, one 4" x 7" rectangle and one 4" x 6" rectangle for buildings, and one 2" x 3" rectangle and one 2" square for building doors. Trace two rooftops on Wonder-Under side of orange fabric. Cut out along pattern lines.

5. From red fabric, cut following: two 4" squares for houses, three 1½" x 2½" rectangles for house doors, one 4" x 8" rectangle and one 4" x 6" rectangle for buildings, one 2" x 4" rectangle and one 1½" x 2½" rectangle for building doors. Trace two rooftops on Wonder-Under side of orange fabric. Cut out along pattern lines.

6. From yellow fabric, cut following: two 4" squares for houses and two 1½" x 2½" rectangles for house doors. Trace two rooftops on Wonder-Under side of yellow fabric. Cut out along pattern lines.

7. Trace nine treetops on Wonder-Under side of green vinyl. Cut out along pattern lines. Trace nine tree trunks on Wonder-Under side of black vinyl. Cut out along pattern lines.

8. Referring to photo, position house and rooftop appliqués on play mat. Place house pieces approximately 12" apart along two edges of play mat. First and last house in each row should be 3" from edges of play mat. Tips of roofs should be 1½" from edges of play mat. Remove paper backings. Fuse houses and rooftops in place.

9. Position doors on houses. Remove paper backings. Fuse doors in place. Using royal blue thread, satin-stitch edges of doors, houses, and rooftops. Or, if you prefer, using royal blue fabric paint, outline edges of doors,

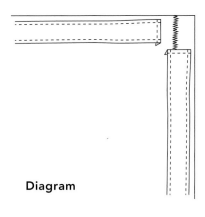

Diagram

houses, and rooftops. Sew one blue round button in place on each door for doorknob.

10. Referring to photo, position one tree between each house. Position three trees, equally spaced, along one blank edge of play mat. Remove paper backings. Pin pieces in place. Turn play mat to wrong side and fuse tree pieces in place. (Remove pins carefully before fusing to avoid disturbing position of appliqués.) Working from right side of play mat and using matching thread, zigzag over edges of treetops and tree trunks. Or, if you prefer, use green and black fabric paint to outline edges of treetops and tree trunks.

11. For city green, from green fabric, cut one 19½" x 21½" piece. Turn raw edges under ½" and press. Referring to photo, position building appliqués on city green. Remove paper backings and fuse buildings in place. Position building doors on buildings. Remove paper backings and fuse doors in place. Using royal blue thread, satin-stitch edges of buildings and doors. Or, if you prefer, use royal blue fabric paint to outline edges of doors and buildings. Sew yellow square buttons in place on each building for windows.

12. For parking lot, from remaining green fabric, cut one 8" x 19½" piece. On right side of parking lot, using narrow-width zigzag, center and stitch ⅛"-wide yellow ribbon along length; cut ribbon. Beginning 3" from one short end of parking lot, stitch remaining ribbon across parking lot, crossing center line; cut ribbon. Stitch five more crosswise yellow ribbon lines on parking lot in same manner,

To store the play mat, simply pile the cars in the center and pull the drawstring. Everything is in one place and ready for the next afternoon of fun.

leaving 2½" between lines. To finish raw edges of parking lot, turn under ½"; press.

13. Referring to photo, center city green on play mat. Topstitch along folded edges of city green. Topstitch again ½" from first topstitching. Position and topstitch parking lot on play mat in same manner.

14. To make road, using narrow-width zigzag, center and stitch ¼"-wide green ribbon on 3"-wide yellow ribbon. Cut road into four equal lengths. Referring to photo,

place one length of road approximately 3" from outer edge of city green. Position remaining three lengths of road around city green in same manner, lapping cut ends. Edgestitch along each side of ribbon road. Satin-stitch any exposed cut ends of ribbon road.

15. Insert cording through casing on back side of play mat. Knot cording ends together. Pull cording ends to close play mat.

hottip
steam helps

The steam created by ironing a damp press cloth helps Wonder-Under's adhesive to penetrate your fabric. If an appliqué isn't bonding properly, use the press cloth as a timing and temperature device. A damp cloth should be dry after 10–15 seconds, the recommended fusing time. Increase the heat if necessary to get a secure bond.

TREETOP

ROOFTOP

TREE TRUNK

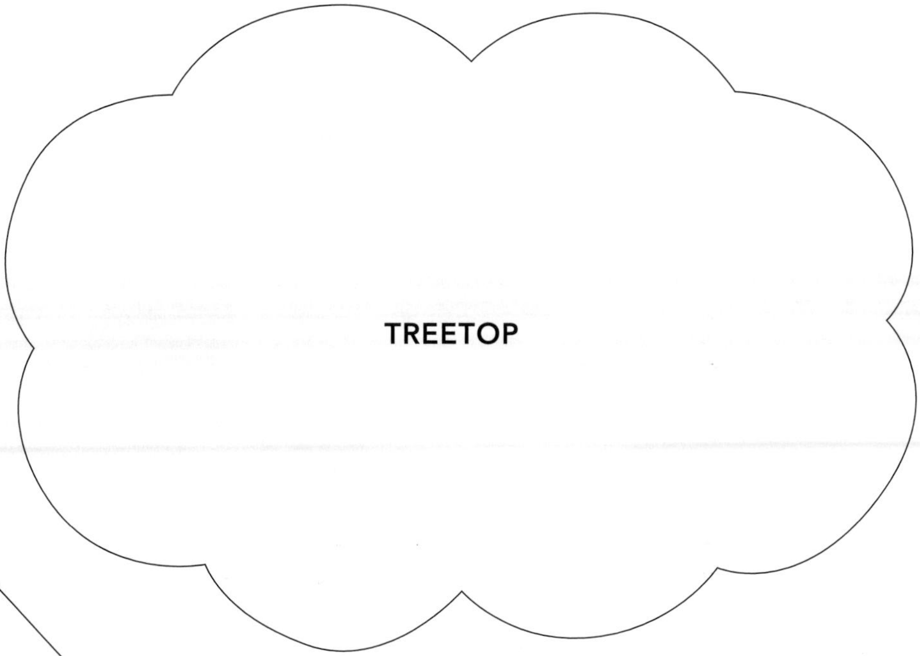

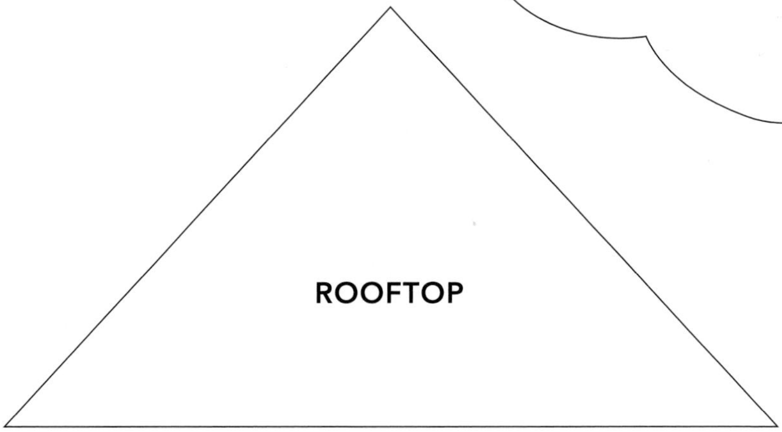

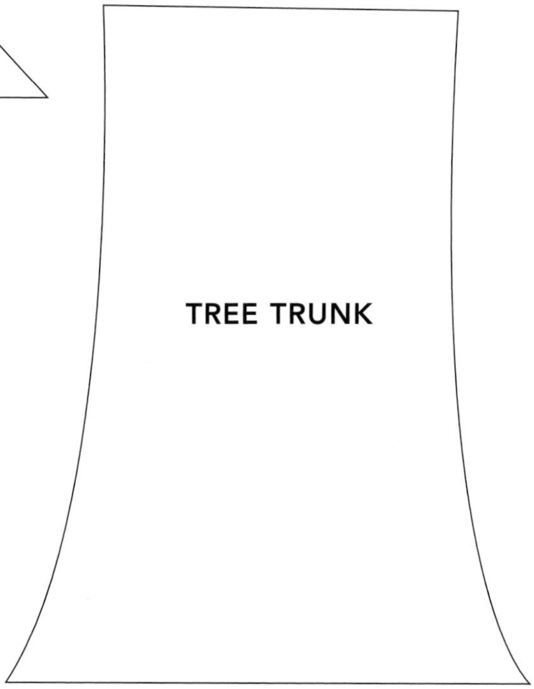

Tooth Fairy Kitty

When your child loses her first tooth, give her this tooth fairy kitty. She'll think you're the cat's meow. Tell her to tuck the tooth in one of the front heart pockets, and the next morning a surprise will appear in its place.

materials

¼ yard mottled beige fabric

Thread: white, yellow

Pellon® Wonder-Under® scraps

Fabric scraps: black-and-white check for collar, red print for dress, yellow solid for socks, black solid for shoes and face, blue print for large hearts, blue solid for small hearts

White tacky glue

½ yard narrow rickrack

Stuffing

¼ yard narrow lace

⅓ yard ¼"-wide black satin ribbon

Permanent black fabric marker

Black carpet thread

Powdered blusher

Hot-glue gun and glue sticks

½ yard ⅝"-wide red grosgrain ribbon

7" square cotton batiste

Instructions

1. From mottled beige fabric, cut two 8" x 11" pieces and two 5" squares. Trace body pattern on wrong side of one 8" x 11" piece. Trace head pattern on wrong side of one 5" square. Machine-stitch along drawn lines. Iron marked pieces. Set head piece aside.

2. Referring to Appliqué-tions on page 10, press Wonder-Under onto wrong side of each fabric scrap, except blue solid. Do not remove paper backings. Referring to photo for colors, trace collar, dress, sock, and shoe patterns on Wonder-Under side of corresponding fabric scraps. Cut out shapes slightly inside drawn lines. Remove paper backings. Positioning appliqués approximately 1/16" inside stitched lines, fuse shapes to right side of body in following order: dress, collar, socks, and shoes.

3. Glue rickrack to collar edges with tacky glue. Trace large heart pattern twice on Wonder-Under side of blue print. Cut out hearts along marked lines. Remove paper backings. Fuse hearts to tips of collar. Trace two small hearts on right side of blue solid. Cut out hearts. Center one small heart, faceup, on top of each large heart. Referring to photo and stitching close to edge, use yellow thread to hand-sew small hearts on large hearts, leaving top edges open.

4. Cut two 5" x 6" pieces from mottled beige fabric. With right sides facing, fold one fabric piece in half lengthwise. Trace arm pattern on wrong side of folded fabric. Machine-stitch through both layers along drawn line, leaving areas indicated on pattern open. Leaving ⅜" seam allowance, cut out arm. Clip curves and turn right side out. Repeat with remaining 5" x 6" piece of mottled beige fabric to make other arm. With right sides facing, align dashed line on one arm with stitching line at one arm opening on body. Stitch along previous stitching line. Repeat to attach other arm to opposite side of body.

5. With right sides facing and edges aligned, place appliquéd body, with arms folded to inside, on top of remaining 8" x 11" mottled beige fabric piece. Using previous stitching line as guide, stitch pieces together, leaving one arm opening unstitched. Leaving ⅜" seam allowance, cut out body. Clip curves and turn right side out. Fill body and arms with stuffing. Turn seam allowances at openings under and slipstitch closed.

6. Hand-stitch division between legs. Use tacky glue to glue lace across top of socks. Cut black ribbon in half. Tie each length in bow. Use tacky glue to glue one bow to top of each shoe.

7. Trace eyes and nose on Wonder-Under side of remaining black fabric scraps. Cut out shapes along pattern lines. Remove paper backings. Referring to photo and patterns, fuse eyes and nose in place on cat head. Using black marker, draw facial details.

8. With right sides facing and edges aligned, place appliquéd head on top of remaining 5" mottled beige fabric square. Using previous stitching line as guide, stitch pieces together, leaving open where indicated on pattern.

Leaving ⅜" seam allowance, cut out head. Clip curves and turn right side out. Fill head with stuffing. Turn seam allowances at opening under and slipstitch closed. For whiskers, using three strands of carpet thread, stitch through cheeks. Tie knots in thread near head. Trim thread to desired length. Use powdered blusher to make cheeks.

9. Using hot-glue gun, glue bottom half of head in place at top of body. Tie grosgrain ribbon in bow. Hot-glue bow to neck.

10. For wings, cut one 3½" x 7" piece of Wonder-Under. Fuse Wonder-Under to one half of batiste. Remove paper backing. Fold batiste in half, sandwiching Wonder-Under between layers. Fuse layers of batiste together. Trace wing pattern on batiste. Using white thread, satin-stitch along marked line. Cut out wings close to stitching. Satin-stitch outer edges of wings again with slightly wider setting to fill in stitches and cover raw edges. Hot-glue wings to back of body.

Bold dashes indicate drawn lines.

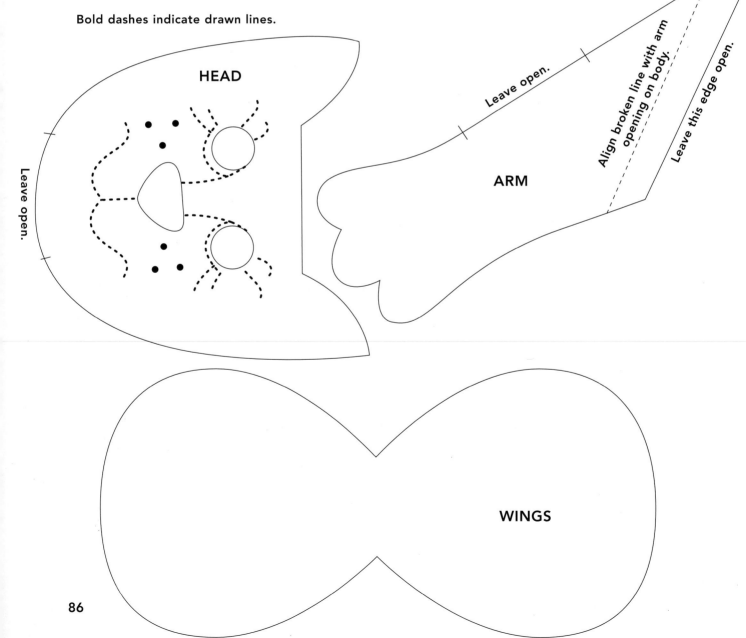

86

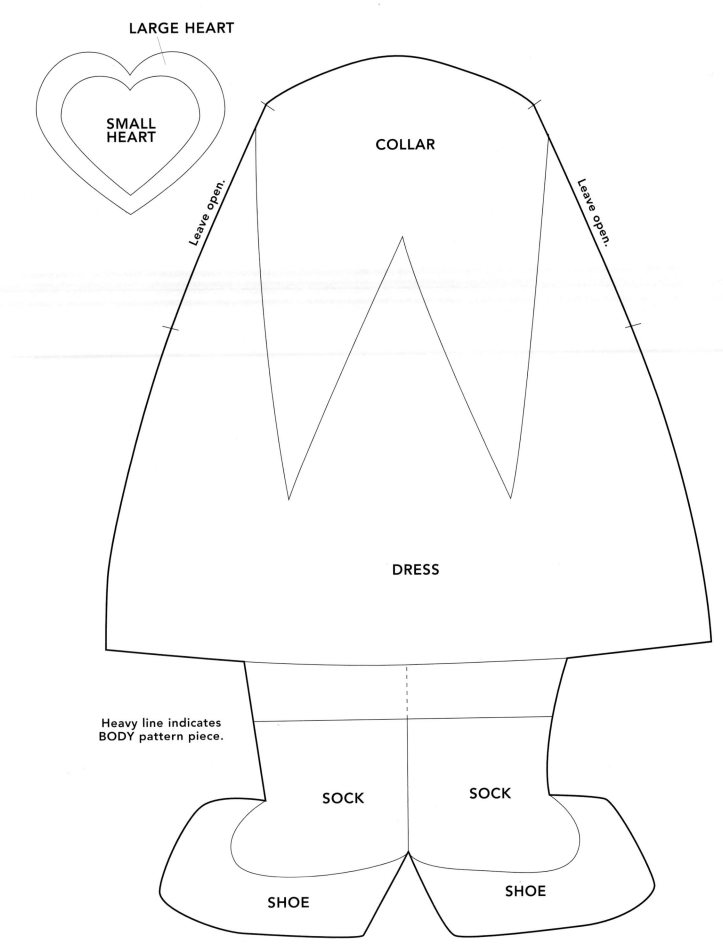

LARGE HEART

SMALL HEART

COLLAR

Leave open.

Leave open.

DRESS

Heavy line indicates
BODY pattern piece.

SOCK

SOCK

SHOE

SHOE

Sock Hop Slippers

Your daughter can cuddle with a kitty cat, ladybug, or little green turtle when she pulls on these colorful socks. Because these citrus-colored slippers are such fun to wear around the house, there will be no more ruined white dress socks.

materials

For each

Disappearing-ink fabric marker

Pellon® Wonder-Under®: 5" x 10" piece, scraps

1 (5" x 10") piece each muslin and fleece

Green puffy fabric paint

For cat

2 (5" x 10") pieces purple-and-black print fabric

Orange fabric scrap

Orange thread

2 small bells

1 pair pink socks

For turtle

2 (5" x 10") pieces green pindot fabric

Thread: bright pink, black

4 black seed beads

1 pair orange socks

For ladybug

2 (5" x 10") pieces red fabric

Black fabric scrap

Thread: black, pink

4 black seed beads

1 pair yellow socks

Instructions

1. For cat: Positioning pattern near one short end of fabric rectangle and using disappearing-ink fabric marker, trace cat pattern on right side of one purple-and-black print piece. Reverse pattern and trace on opposite end of same rectangle. Referring to Appliqué-tions on page 10, and with edges aligned, press Wonder-Under rectangle onto wrong side of marked purple-and-black rectangle. Do not remove paper backing.

2. Press Wonder-Under scrap onto wrong side of orange fabric scrap. On paper side of Wonder-Under, trace each shaded detail twice. Cut out detail shapes along pattern lines. Remove paper backing from details. Referring to photo and pattern, fuse details to right side of each cat. Remove paper backing from decorated purple-and-black rectangle.

3. Fuse muslin rectangle to wrong side of decorated purple-and-black rectangle. Stack remaining purple-and-black print piece (right side

down), one fleece piece, and cat piece (right side up). Baste. Using narrow satin stitch and orange thread, and referring to pattern, satin-stitch around edges of details, along stitching lines, and around outer edges of each cat. Cut out cats, being careful not to clip stitches. Using wider stitch and orange thread, satin-stitch around edges again to fill in stitches and cover raw edges.

4. Referring to pattern and Diagram E on page 56 and using orange thread, straightstitch eyes. Stitch one bell to center of each cat's neck. Stitch one cat to each pink sock. To help keep socks from slipping on floor, make four rows of dots on bottom of each sock with puffy paint.

5. For turtle: To make two turtle appliqués, repeat steps 1-3, using bright pink thread for satin stitching and omitting fabric details. Referring to pattern, satin-stitch cheeks. Referring to Diagram E on page 56, straightstitch nose on each turtle with pink thread. For eyes, stitch

two beads to each turtle. Stitch one turtle to each orange sock. Make four rows of dots on bottom of each sock with puffy paint.

6. For ladybug: To make two ladybug appliqués, repeat steps 1–3, using black thread for satin stitching and black fabric scrap for details. Referring to pattern, satin-stitch cheeks with pink thread. For eyes, stitch two black beads to each ladybug. Stitch one ladybug to each yellow sock. Make four rows of dots on bottom of each sock with puffy paint.

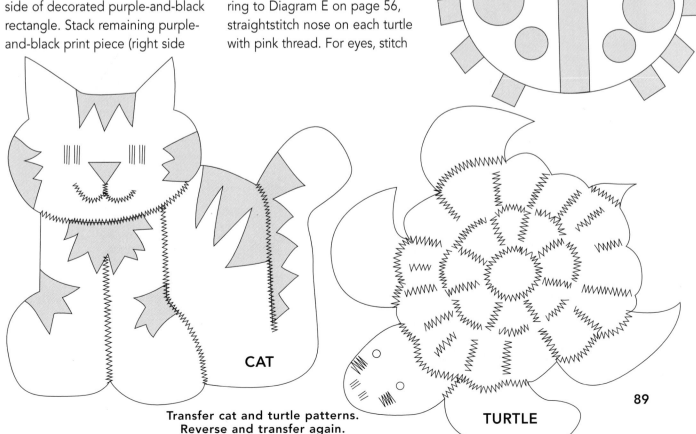

LADYBUG

CAT

TURTLE

Transfer cat and turtle patterns.
Reverse and transfer again.

Belly Bags

Children on the go can keep all of their important belongings front and center with these adorable belly bags.

materials

For each

Disappearing-ink fabric marker

½ yard Pellon® Wonder-Under®

12" square muslin

6" x 12" piece of fleece

For raccoon

⅓ yard yellow nylon fabric

Teal nylon fabric scraps

Teal thread

2 (⅜)" sew-on wiggle eyes

Purple fanny pack

For beaver

⅓ yard pink nylon fabric

Orange nylon fabric scraps

Pink thread

2 (⅜") sew-on wiggle eyes

Red fanny pack

For snail

⅓ yard orange nylon fabric

Teal nylon fabric scraps

Thread: teal, yellow

1 (⅜") sew-on wiggle eye

Blue fanny pack

Designed by Linda Hendrickson

Instructions

1. From ⅓ yard nylon fabric, cut one 12" square. Using disappearing-ink fabric marker, trace desired animal's outline to right side of fabric, ½" from bottom edge. From Wonder-Under, cut one 12" square. Referring to Appliqué-tions on page 10, and with edges aligned, press Wonder-Under square onto wrong side of nylon fabric square. Do not remove paper backing.

2. Press Wonder-Under onto wrong side of fabric scraps used for details. Referring to photo, on paper side of Wonder-Under, trace following details: For raccoon, trace eyes, nose, and tail stripes; for beaver, trace ears, nose, and tail; for snail, trace shell. Cut out shapes along pattern lines. Remove paper backing. Referring to photo and patterns, fuse details onto right side of animal.

3. Remove paper backing from decorated nylon square. Fuse muslin square to wrong side of nylon square. With muslin sides facing, fold square in half, sandwiching fleece between layers. Pin, then baste layers together.

4. Referring to patterns, for each animal, satin-stitch along zigzagged stitching lines. Then, for raccoon, satin-stitch around eyes, nose, and along teal tail stripes; for beaver, satin-stitch around ears and nose. Satin-stitch outline of animal shape. Cut out animal shape close to stitching. Satin-stitch outer edges of animal again with slightly wider setting to fill in stitches and cover raw edges.

5. Hand-sew wiggle eyes in place. Unzip bag. Pin center of animal to center front of bag, catching top layer only. Topstitch around sides and bottom of animal, leaving opening between Xs to create another pocket.

RACCOON

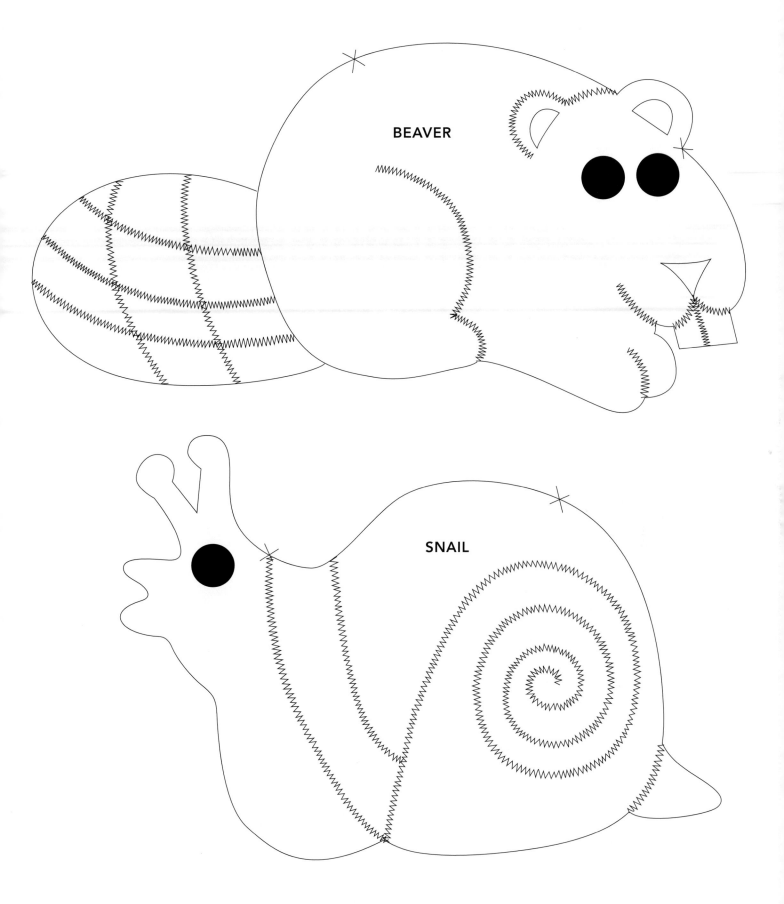

BEAVER

SNAIL

Gym Shorts Laundry Bag

Hang this appliquéd canvas bag from a hook on the back of your child's door.
Then she'll know exactly where to deposit her grass-stained soccer or softball uniforms.

materials

1 yard Pellon® Wonder-Under®

45"-wide fabric: ⅛ yard white, ⅛ yard red, ⅛ yard flesh color, ¼ yard red-and-white stripe, ⅔ yard blue

Thread to match fabrics

2 yards thick white cotton cording

Instructions

Finished Size: Approximately 22" square

1. Trace two shoes, two of each shoelace, two of each bow, two of each patch, and two shoe soles onto paper side of Wonder-Under. Trace gym shorts and leg onto paper side of Wonder-Under. Reverse leg pattern and trace again. Leaving approximately ½" margin, cut around each shape, except gym shorts. Cut out gym shorts along pattern line.

2. Referring to Appliqué-tions on page 10, press following Wonder-Under shapes onto wrong side of white fabric: shoelaces, bows, patches, and shoe soles. Press Wonder-Under shoes onto wrong side of red fabric. Press Wonder-Under leg shapes onto wrong side of flesh-color fabric. (Do not press Wonder-Under gym shorts onto fabric yet.) Cut out shapes along pattern lines. Remove paper backing.

3. Trace gym shorts pattern onto wrong side of red-and-white stripe fabric. Cut out gym shorts along pattern lines. To cuff leg of shorts, turn bottom edge of one leg under ¼". Press to wrong side and stitch. Turn leg under again 1½" and press to wrong side. Fold up cuff 1" to right side of shorts and press. Repeat for other leg. Place Wonder-Under shorts on wrong side of fabric shorts. Trim Wonder-Under shorts to match. Press Wonder-Under shorts to wrong side of fabric shorts. Remove paper backing.

4. With right side faceup, lay blue fabric on flat surface so that one 45" edge is at top. Referring to Diagram, position legs on blue fabric. (It may help to position shorts on top of legs to get accurate placement. Remove shorts before fusing legs.) Fuse legs in place. Referring to photo, fuse all shoe pieces and shoelaces in place. Using medium zigzag stitch, zigzag along edges of each piece.

5. With right sides faceup and top edges aligned, position shorts on blue fabric. Using medium zigzag stitch, zigzag along inner and outer

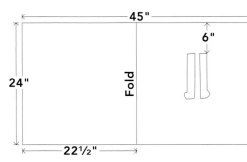

45"

6"

24"

Fold

22½"

Diagram

edges of shorts. (Do not stitch bottom or top edges of shorts.)

6. To make bag casing, turn top edge of blue fabric under ½" and press to wrong side. Turn edge under 1½" again and press to wrong side. Stitch close to edge of first fold.

7. With right sides facing and edges aligned, fold blue fabric in half widthwise. Using ½" seam, stitch bottom and side edges, leaving ends of casing free. Turn bag right side out and press. Pull cording through casing. Knot ends of cording.

Place on fold.

GYM SHORTS

other ideas

Before sending your child off to summer camp, stitch him a gym shorts laundry bag, then create a matching personalized sleeping bag. Fuse the shorts, shoe, and leg appliqués to the lower half of the sleeping bag, then cut out a shirt, arms, and head from fabric. Fuse the appliqués to the bag, just above the shorts. Seal edges of appliqués with fabric paint. Use fabric paint to add hair and a face.

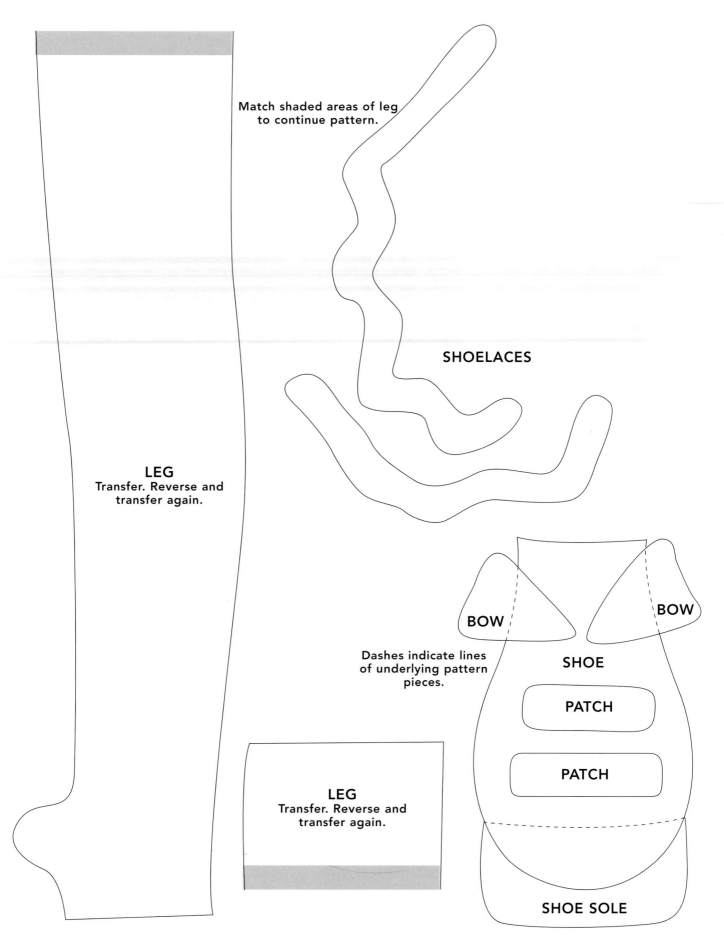

Match shaded areas of leg
to continue pattern.

SHOELACES

LEG
Transfer. Reverse and
transfer again.

Dashes indicate lines
of underlying pattern
pieces.

BOW

BOW

SHOE

PATCH

PATCH

LEG
Transfer. Reverse and
transfer again.

SHOE SOLE

Darling Doll Dress

Let Patchwork Patrick and Mop Top Molly accompany your little girl wherever she goes. "What a doll!" people will say, when she wears a denim jumper decorated with this delightful duo.

materials

¼ yard Pellon® Heavy Duty Wonder-Under®

Fabric scraps: blue, cream-and-red stripe, red print, red plaid, red-and-cream miniplaid, white with tiny red stars, flesh color for faces, red pindot

2 (5" x 12") muslin pieces

Purchased denim jumper

Thread: red, black, white

Permanent fabric markers: red, black

4 black seed beads

4 white beads

3 (¼") white buttons

Instructions

Note: Use muslin rectangles as bases for building doll appliqués.
1. Referring to Appliqué-tions on page 10, press Wonder-Under onto wrong side of fabric scraps. Do not remove paper backing. Referring to photo for fabric

Designed by Linda Hendrickson

reference, trace pattern pieces on Wonder-Under side of fabric scraps. Cut out shapes along pattern lines. Remove paper backings.
2. Referring to photo and pattern, position girl pieces on one muslin rectangle and boy pieces on remaining muslin rectangle. Fuse pieces in place.
3. Press Wonder-Under onto wrong side of muslin rectangles. Cut out doll shapes. Remove paper backings. Position dolls on

front of jumper. Fuse dolls in place. Satin-stitch edges of each shape with red thread.
4. Referring to pattern, draw star eyes and dot nostrils on dolls using black fabric marker; draw mouth using red fabric marker. Using black thread, sew one black seed bead in place on top of each drawn star eye. Using white thread, stitch white beads in place on girl's dress; stitch buttons in place on boy's overalls.

other ideas

For an alternative fusible fashion, apply Patchwork Patrick and Mop Top Molly to the legs of a pair of jeans just below the knees. Or appliqué Patrick or Molly to your children's bath towels to designate his and hers towels.

Dashes indicate lines of underlying pattern pieces.

Overlap shaded areas of boy to continue pattern.

×
× Button
placement
×

BOY

hottip
temporarily tacky

Before fusing, you can "baste" an appliqué in place to see how you like the position. For a temporary bond, place the appliqué on the background fabric and, using the tip of a hot iron, lightly touch the appliqué in various spots. If you decide to move the appliqué, you can lift it up and reposition it. Once the appliqué is exactly where you want it, cover the appliqué with a damp press cloth and permanently fuse.

Overlap shaded areas of girl to continue pattern.

GIRL

Bead placement

Dashes indicate lines of underlying pattern pieces.

Mardi Gras Masks

Designed by Phyllis Dunstan

Adults aren't the only ones who love Mardi Gras. Make these quick-and-easy masks for your kids and their friends. Then order a king cake, put on some jazz music, and host a parade right on your own street! These fabric masks are quite durable and will last long after the last string of beads has been tossed.

materials

For each

Manila folder

½ yard Pellon® Heavy Duty Wonder-Under®

2 eyelets and eyelet punch

1 yard ⅛"-wide satin ribbon

White tacky glue

For chicken

Fabric scraps: yellow, purple, turquoise, white, black, orange

Purple sequins

For clown king

Fabric scraps: purple, yellow, white, light green, red, black

Red acrylic jewels

Instructions for Chicken

Note: Use a dry press cloth for this project.

1. Trace chicken face base pattern onto manila folder and paper side of Wonder-Under. Cut out shapes along pattern lines. Referring to Appliqué-tions on page 10, press Wonder-Under face onto manila folder face. Remove paper backing.

2. Trace face base pattern onto right side of yellow fabric. Cut out shape along pattern lines. Fuse fabric face onto manila folder face. Cut out shaded eye holes.

3. Trace cheek, feather, eye, beak, and nostril patterns on paper side of Wonder-Under. Reverse cheek, feather, eye, and nostril patterns, and trace again. Leaving approximately ¼" margin, cut around

Wonder-Under shapes. Referring to photo for colors, press Wonder-Under shapes onto wrong side of fabric scraps. Cut out along pattern lines. Remove paper backings, except for white eyes. Trace one cheek and one cheek reversed on right side of turquoise scrap. Trace one beak on right side of orange scrap. Cut out cheeks and beak along pattern lines.

4. Fuse matching turquoise cheeks together. Fuse beaks together. Fold beak in half and crease with iron. Referring to photo, fuse purple cheeks on top of turquoise cheeks, fuse nostrils on beak, and fuse black eyes on top of white eyes. Remove paper backing from white eyes. Fuse feathers and eyes on face base.

5. Cut small pieces of Wonder-Under in shape of shaded areas on cheek and beak. Press corresponding Wonder-Under pieces to backs of cheeks and beak. Remove paper backing. Referring to photo, fuse cheeks and beak in place.

6. Referring to photo, glue sequins to mask. Let dry. Using eyelet punch, attach one eyelet to each side of mask just above cheek. Cut ribbon in half. Tie ribbons to eyelets.

Instructions for Clown King

Note: Use a dry press cloth for this project.

1. Trace clown king face base pattern (including crown) onto manila folder and paper side of Wonder-Under. Cut out face shapes along pattern lines. Referring to Appliqué-tions on page 10, press Wonder-Under face onto manila

folder face. Remove paper backing.

2. Refer to Step 2 for Chicken to apply purple crown and white face to manila folder face.

3. Referring to Step 3 for Chicken, trace crown decorations, eyebrow, tear, cheek, and mustache patterns on paper side of Wonder-Under. Leaving approximately ¼" margin, cut around Wonder-Under shapes. Referring to photo for colors, press Wonder-Under shapes onto wrong side of fabric scraps. Cut out shapes along pattern lines. Remove paper backings, except for black eyebrow shapes and black tear shapes.

4. Trace one mustache on right side of black fabric. Cut out along pattern lines. Fuse mustaches together. Cut two small pieces of Wonder-Under in shape of shaded areas on mustache. Press Wonder-Under pieces to back of mustache in shaded areas. Remove paper backings.

5. Center and fuse colored eyebrow pieces and colored tear pieces on top of corresponding black pieces. Remove paper backings from black pieces. Referring to photo, fuse all appliqués in place.

6. Refer to Step 6 for Chicken to glue gems on mask and attach eyelets and ribbon.

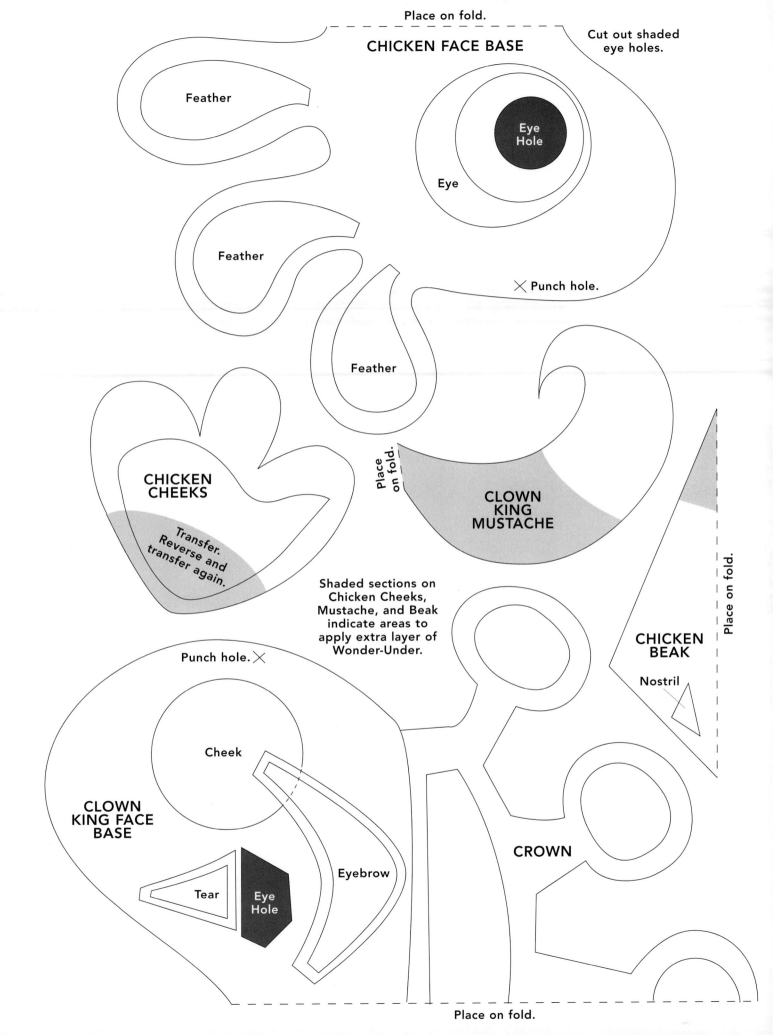

Travel Gear

Designed by Linda Hendrickson

These directional appliqués point your kids toward fun as they set off for adventure with their trusty travel gear. Because the appliqués make the luggage readily identifiable, their bags will be easy to locate in crowded airports.

materials

1 yard Pellon® Wonder-Under®

Fabric scraps in desired colors

Purchased garment bag, tote bag, and toiletry bag

Fabric paints in desired colors

Plastic garbage bag

Hand-sewing needle

Thread to match fabric for luggage tag

3 star buttons

Instructions

Note: Adjust sizes of embellishments or their placement depending upon sizes of purchased bags.

1. Determine desired number and placement of shapes. Trace arrows (except luggage tag pattern), star, and circle patterns onto paper side of Wonder-Under as many times as desired. Leaving approximately ½" margin, cut around shapes. Referring to Appliqué-tions on page 10, press Wonder-Under shapes onto wrong side of fabric scraps. Cut out fabric shapes along pattern lines. Remove paper backing.

2. Fuse shapes on each bag in desired positions. Outline shapes with fabric paint to seal appliqué edges. Add dot and squiggle embellishments if desired. Let paint dry.

3. To make luggage tags, trace luggage tag pattern onto paper side of Wonder-Under. Leaving approximately ½" margin, cut around shape. Press Wonder-Under shape onto wrong side of fabric scrap. Cut out shape along pattern line. Remove paper backing. Trace luggage tag pattern onto wrong side of remainder of fabric scrap. Cut out shape along pattern line. With wrong sides facing and edges aligned, fuse luggage tag pieces together. Cover table with plastic bag to protect surface. Using fabric paint, outline one side of tag. Write child's name on tag. Include address and phone number if desired. Let paint dry. Turn tag over and outline opposite side. Let paint dry. Wrap tag around one bag handle and hand-sew tag layers together. Secure with one star button.

LUGGAGE TAG

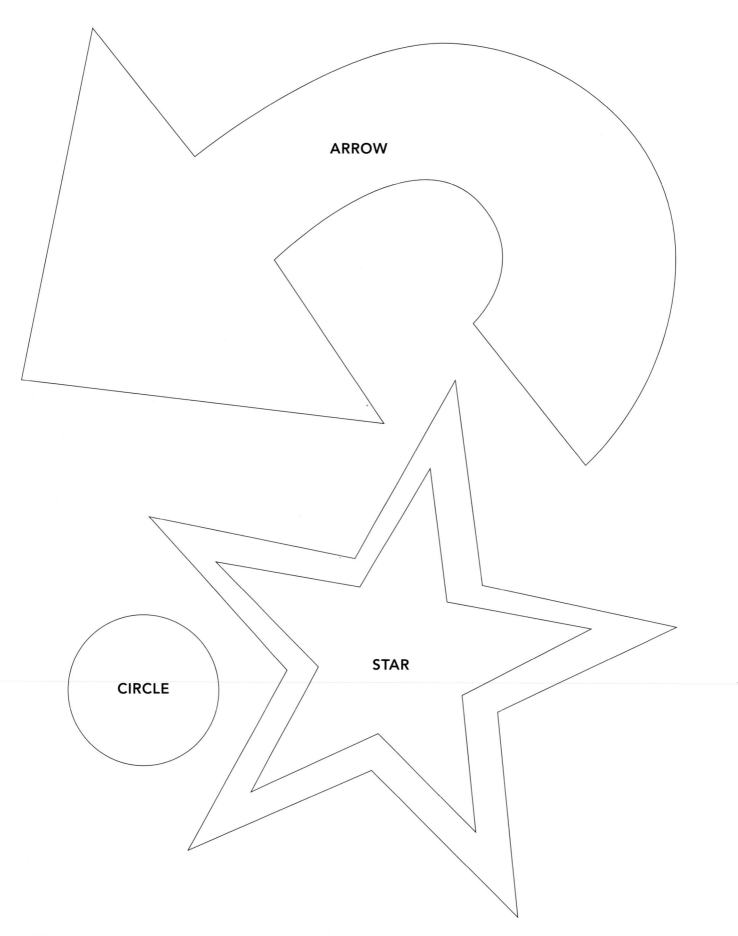

ARROW

STAR

CIRCLE

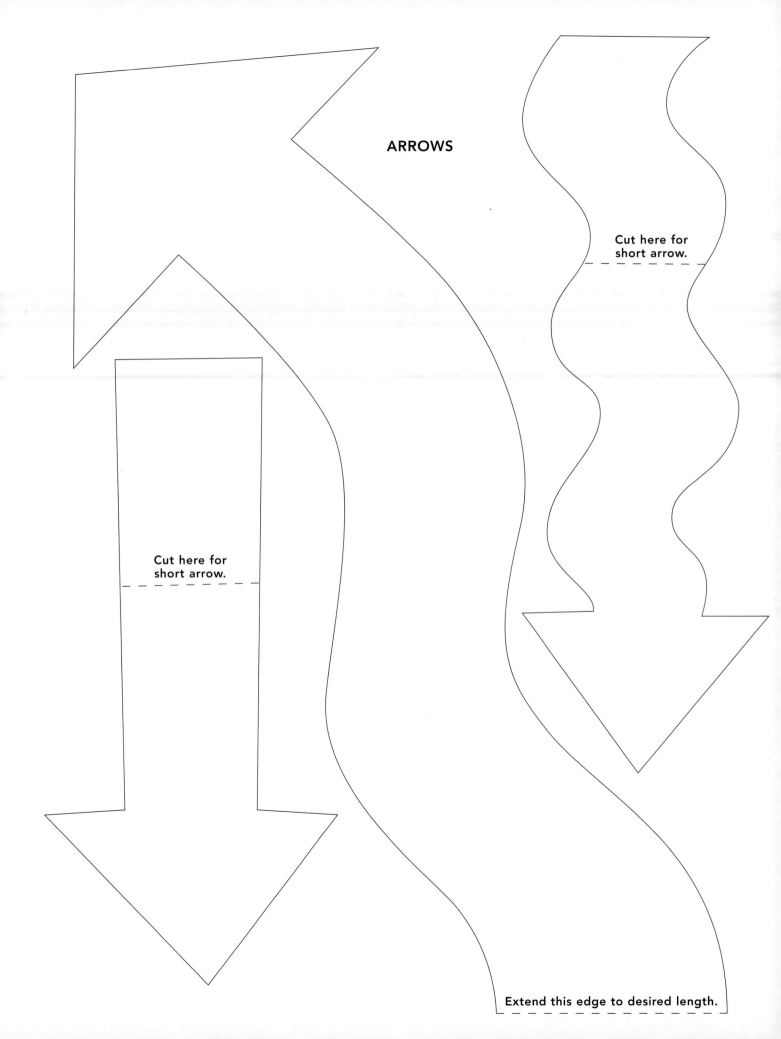

ARROWS

Cut here for
short arrow.

Cut here for
short arrow.

Extend this edge to desired length.

page 136

page 115

page 134

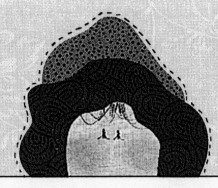

Year-Round Wonders

Appliqués celebrating Easter, the arrival of a new baby, Halloween, Thanksgiving, and Christmas are all found in this chapter. When your family gathers for its next special occasion, these projects will help set the mood for the festivities that follow.

IT'S A BABY!

Designed by Linda Hendrickson

Special Delivery Banner

It's a banner occasion when a baby is born! Fly this stork from a flagpole to announce that your special delivery has finally arrived, or display the banner at a baby shower. The basket is removable, so you can make one for a boy and another for a girl, then switch them accordingly.

materials

45"-wide fabric: ⅔ yard for background; ½ yard for stork body and neck; ⅓ yard for legs and tail feathers; ¼ yard for tail feather, wing, and head; ¼ yard for beak and knees; 2 (2" x 10") strips for basket hanger; 6" x 8" piece for each basket; scraps for each baby head and blanket

1⅛ yard fusible interfacing

Thread to match background fabric

String

Pushpin

Large piece kraft paper for patterns

2 yards Pellon® Wonder-Under®

Puffy fabric paint in coordinating color

4 (½") buttons

Rice

¼ yard muslin

Finished size: 21" x 42½" (including legs)

Instructions

Note: Seam allowances are ¼".

1. From background fabric and interfacing, cut two 21½" x 19½" pieces each. Press interfacing pieces onto wrong sides of background pieces.

2. From remaining background fabric, cut one 3" x 20" strip for banner hanger. To hem edges of hanger, turn both short ends under ¼" twice and stitch; turn one long edge under ¼" twice and stitch. With raw edges aligned, center banner hanger strip faceup on right side of one background fabric piece. Edgestitch along finished long edge of banner hanger, backstitching at beginning and end. Set background piece aside.

3. To make body pattern, tie one end of string to point end of pencil. Insert pushpin through string 6¾" from attached pencil. Insert pushpin into center of kraft paper. Holding string taut, mark circle on paper. Cut out circle. To make wing pattern, remove pushpin from string and reinsert it 3" from attached pencil. Draw circle on kraft paper as before. Draw cutting line at 5⅛" across top half of circle. Cut out circle. To make knee pattern, remove pushpin from string and reinsert it ⅞" from attached pencil. Draw circle on paper as before. Cut out circle. To make beak pattern, draw one 4⅝" x 7⅞" rectangle. Draw diagonal line from upper left corner to lower right corner. Cut out right triangle.

4. Trace one body, one wing, one neck, one head, one beak, four knees, and one of each tail feather onto paper side of Wonder-Under. Leaving approximately ½" margin, cut around shapes. Referring to Appliqué-tions on page 10, press Wonder-Under shapes onto corresponding fabrics. Cut out fabric shapes along pattern lines. Remove paper backings.

5. Referring to photo, arrange body, neck, head, beak, and tail feather appliqués on right side of background piece without hanger. Fuse pieces in place. Position wing on body and fuse. Edgestitch around appliqués. Embellish wing and tail feathers with fabric paint. Let dry. Sew one button on head for eye.

6. To make legs and talons, cut four 2½" x 24" strips, and four 2½" x 11" strips from fabric for legs. Press interfacing onto wrong side of each rectangle. For legs, with right sides facing and raw edges aligned, stitch long edges and one short edge of each pair of 2½" x 24" strips. Turn strips right side out and press. Pour one tablespoon of rice into each leg. For talons, stitch and fill each pair of 2½" x 11" strips as above. Slipstitch open end of each talon

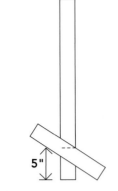

5"

Diagram

closed. Divide rice between each end of talon; fold each talon in

half. Referring to Diagram, lay one talon over bottom of each leg, making an X. Stitch a straight line where the two intersect. Fold top half of each talon down.

7. Measure, and mark 8" down from top of each leg. On one leg, center two knees, one on either side of leg, on 8" mark. Fuse knees to leg and to each other. Repeat to attach remaining knees to other leg. With raw edges aligned, center and pin legs, side-by-side, to right side of base of stork body.

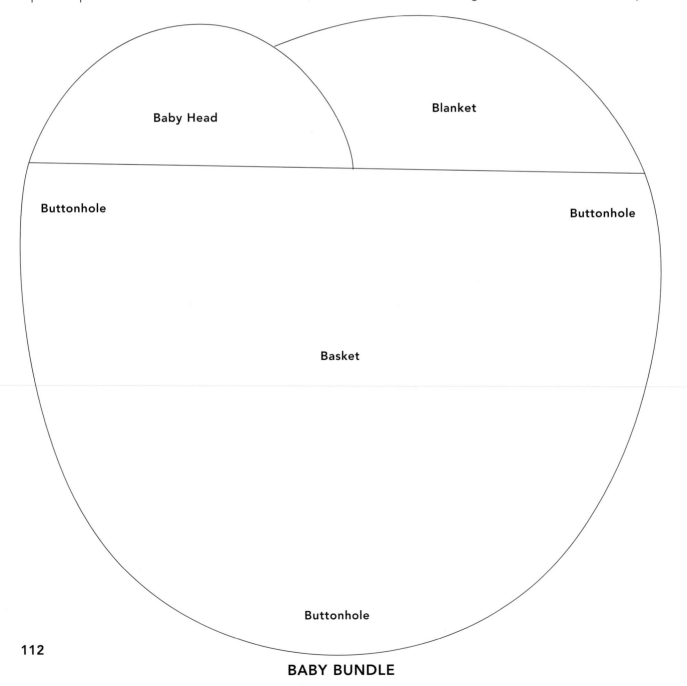

Baby Head

Blanket

Buttonhole

Buttonhole

Basket

Buttonhole

BABY BUNDLE

8. To assemble banner, with right sides facing and raw edges aligned, stitch appliquéd banner background to hanger background piece, leaving a 4" opening on one side. Make sure hanger is at top of banner and legs are folded away from seam line. Turn banner right side out and press. Slipstitch opening closed.

9. Trace baby bundle (including baby head, blanket, and basket) on muslin and on interfacing. Cut out. Press interfacing shape onto right side of corresponding muslin shape. Trace basket, baby head, and blanket onto paper side of Wonder-Under. Leaving approximately ½" margin, cut around shapes. Press Wonder-Under shapes onto corresponding fabrics. Cut out shapes along pattern lines. Remove paper backings. Position pieces on muslin and fuse. Stitch three buttonholes where indicated on basket pattern. Using fabric paint, write "It's A Boy!", "It's A Girl!", or "It's A Baby!".

10. For basket hanger, cut two 1" x 10" lengths of Wonder-Under. With one long edge aligned, press one Wonder-Under strip onto wrong side of each 2" x 10" fabric strip. Remove paper backings. With wrong sides facing, fold each strip in half lengthwise and fuse. Referring to photo for position and using baby bundle as guide, satin-stitch hangers in place along bottom edge of beak. Sew one button onto each end of hanger through all thicknesses. Sew one button onto bottom of banner, using baby basket as guide for placement.

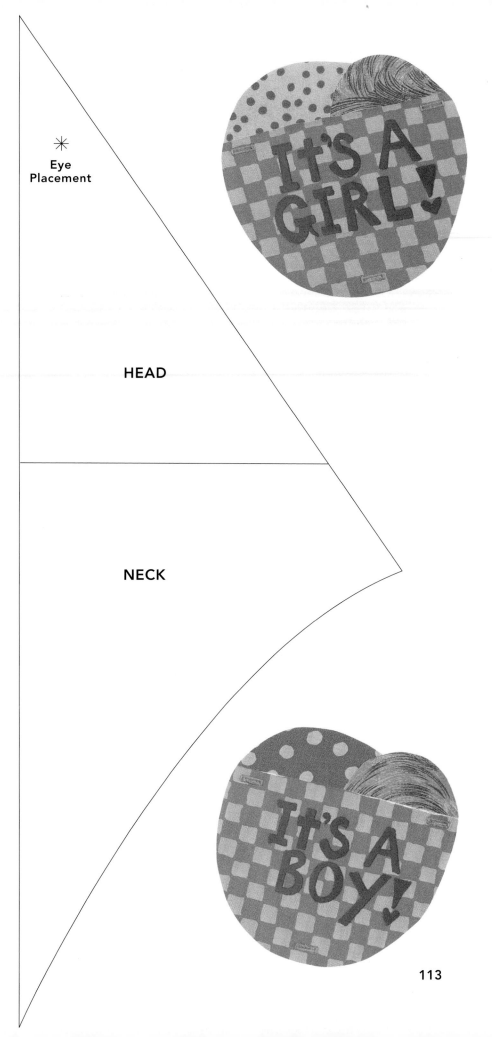

✳
Eye Placement

HEAD

NECK

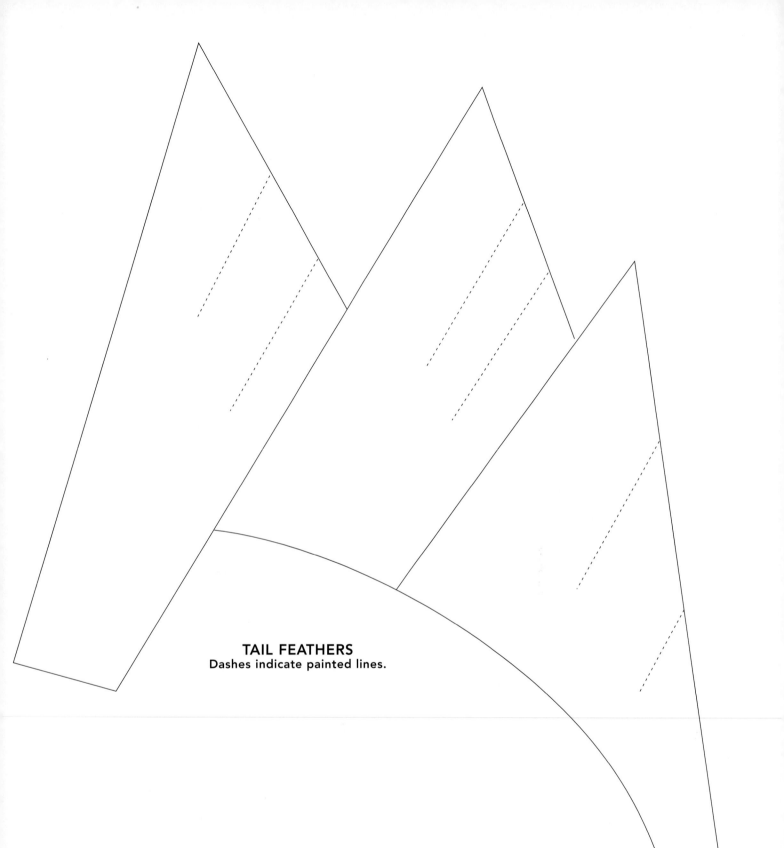

TAIL FEATHERS
Dashes indicate painted lines.

114

Easter Egg Ornaments

Designed by Carol Tipton

Top your holiday table with these enchanting Easter ornaments. Hang them from a branch spray-painted white, or display them in egg cups, as we have done here.

materials

(For one ornament)

Fabric: 7" x 10" piece for egg, scraps for appliqués

7" x 10" piece lightweight batting

Pellon® Wonder-Under® scraps

Permanent black fabric marker (for bunny and chick eggs)

½ yard ⅛"-wide white rickrack

½ yard ⅛"-wide satin ribbon

Finished size: 3½" x 5½"

Instructions

1. Trace egg pattern onto wrong side of 7" x 10" fabric piece and batting piece; cut two each.

2. Trace desired appliqué patterns onto paper side of Wonder-Under. Leaving approximately ½" margin, cut around shapes. Referring to Appliqué-tions on page 10, press Wonder-Under shapes onto wrong side of fabric scraps. Cut out shapes along pattern lines. Remove paper backings.

3. Referring to photo, arrange appliqués on right side of one fabric egg piece. Fuse appliqués in place. For bunny egg, use black fabric marker to draw eye. For chick egg, use black fabric marker to draw eye and legs.

4. With edges aligned, pin rickrack along edge of right side of appliquéd egg front, beginning and ending at top. Machine-baste rickrack in place.

5. With raw edges aligned, layer appliquéd egg front, right side up; egg back, right side down; and two egg-shaped pieces of batting. Stitch layers together along basting line, leaving 2" open at bottom for turning. Turn egg right side out. Fold open edges under and slipstitch closed.

6. Tie ribbon in bow. Sew ribbon bow to top of egg.

other ideas

Bring an added touch of Easter fun to your table by fusing these appliqués to the edges of purchased cloth napkins.

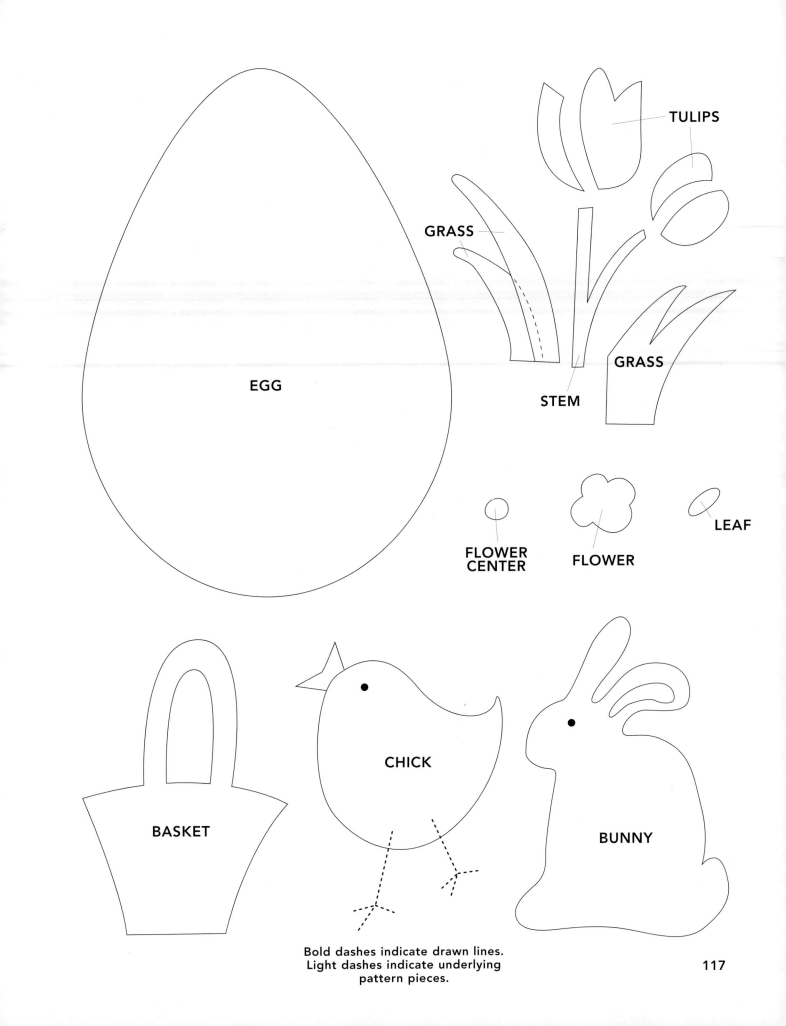

TULIPS

GRASS

GRASS

STEM

EGG

FLOWER
CENTER

FLOWER

LEAF

BASKET

CHICK

BUNNY

Bold dashes indicate drawn lines.
Light dashes indicate underlying
pattern pieces.

117

Haunted Wall Hanging

This spirited wall hanging is frightfully easy to assemble. The clever use of fusible web makes it an entirely no-sew project. Your family and friends will think it's just "boo-tiful."

materials

Lightweight fusible interfacing

Fabric: 1 (28½" x 21") piece for front; 1 (27" x 34½") piece for border; 2 (1" x 21") torn strips; 2 (1" x 28½") torn strips; organdy scrap for ghost; scraps for stars, "Boo", and jack-o'-lanterns; 4" x 27" strip for hanging sleeve

1¼ yard Pellon® Wonder-Under®

1"-wide Wonder-Under fusible tape

Aluminum foil

Pinking shears

Fine-tip permanent black marker

27" length ¼"-diameter dowel

Finished Size: 28½" x 21"

Instructions

1. Fuse interfacing to wrong sides of front fabric piece and border fabric piece. Referring to Appliqué-tions on page 10, press Wonder-Under to wrong side of front fabric piece. Remove paper backing.

2. Cut 3" square from each corner of border fabric piece. Center and fuse front piece to wrong side of border fabric piece.

3. Press fusible tape to wrong sides of torn fabric strips. Remove paper backing. Referring to photo, fuse torn strips to front fabric piece, positioning vertical strips 5½" from sides and horizontal strips 5" from top and from bottom.

4. Press fusible tape along one long edge on wrong side of border fabric piece. Do not remove paper backing. Press edge 3" to wrong side, covering corresponding edge of front fabric piece. Unfold edge and remove paper backing. Refold edge and fuse in place. Repeat for remaining long edge, then short edges of border fabric piece.

5. Trace ghost pattern onto paper side of Wonder-Under. Leaving approximately ½" margin, cut around shape. Cut piece of aluminum foil larger than organdy scrap. Place foil, shiny side up, on ironing board. Layer organdy, wrong side up, on foil; then Wonder-Under shape, paper side up. Press Wonder-Under shape onto wrong side of organdy. Peel organdy away from foil. Cut out shape along pattern lines. Remove and save paper backing.

6. Trace four large stars, four small stars, six leaves, and one each of Jack-o'-lantern A, Jack-o'-lantern B, Jack-o'-lantern C, Stem A, Stem B, and Stem C on paper side of Wonder-Under. Leaving approximately ½" margin, cut around shapes. Referring to photo for colors, press Wonder-Under shapes

onto wrong side of fabric scraps. Cut out shapes along pattern lines. Cut out jack-o'-lantern faces. Remove paper backings.

7. Leaving at least 1" between shapes, draw four 2¼" squares and trace "Boo" onto paper side of Wonder-Under. Leaving approximately ½" margin, cut around shapes. Referring to photo for colors, press Wonder-Under shapes onto wrong side of fabric scraps. Cut out inside of letters along pattern lines, using regular scissors. Cut around outer edges of letters and squares with pinking shears. Remove paper backings.

8. Referring to photo, arrange appliqués on wall hanging. Place saved paper backing piece over ghost. Fuse appliqués in place.

9. Using black fabric marker and referring to photo, draw pen stitching on large stars and details on ghost and jack-o'-lanterns.

10. For hanging sleeve, press all edges of 4" x 27" strip under 1". Press fusible tape onto wrong side of sleeve along each long, pressed edge. Remove paper backings. Center sleeve on back of wall hanging ½" from top. Fuse in place. Insert dowel into sleeve.

LARGE STAR

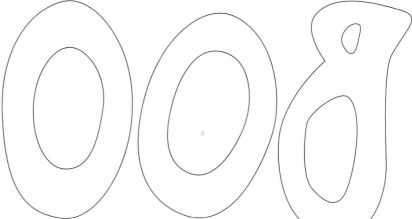

STEM A

JACK-O'-LANTERN A

SMALL STAR

LEAF

GHOST

JACK-O'-LANTERN B

JACK-O'-LANTERN C

120

STEM B

STEM C

Pilgrim Place Mat

This no-sew Thanksgiving place mat will remind everyone at the table why we celebrate the holiday. And it's so easy! Start with a purchased mat, then fuse on the design.

materials

Purchased place mat (at least 12" x 17")

Fabric scraps for appliqués

Pellon® Wonder-Under® scraps

Permanent black marker

Finished size: Approximately 12" x 17"

Instructions

1. Wash and dry place mat and appliqué fabrics; do not use fabric softener in washer or dryer. Press.
2. Referring to Appliqué-tions on page 10, press Wonder-Under onto wrong side of fabric scraps. Do not remove paper backing.

Referring to photo for colors, trace appliqué patterns onto Wonder-Under side of fabric scraps. Cut out fabric shapes along pattern lines. Remove paper backings.
3. Referring to photo and patterns, fuse Wonder-Under shapes to place mat in order indicated on patterns. To finish, using permanent marker, draw eyes and mouth on face.

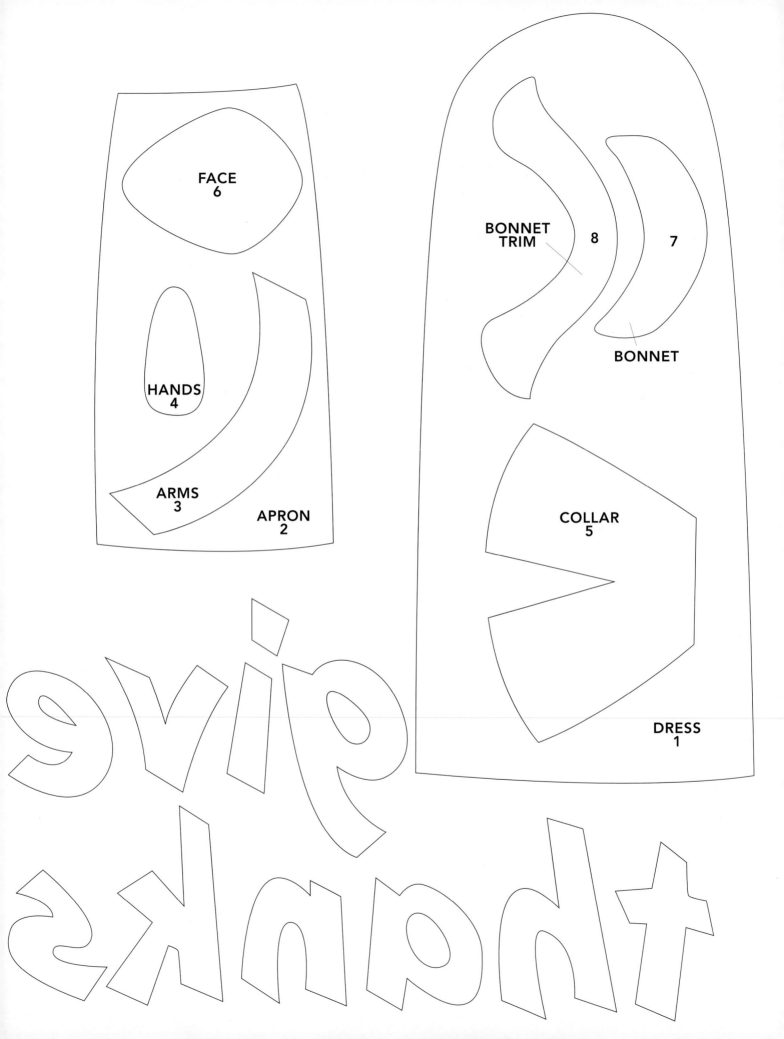

FACE
6

HANDS
4

ARMS
3

APRON
2

BONNET
TRIM

8

7

BONNET

COLLAR
5

DRESS
1

give

thanks

Twittering Tree Skirt

This tree skirt features all the little birds on jaybird street cheerfully decorating their houses for the holidays. You can add detail and dimension to your tree skirt with no extra work, by using novelty print fabrics like ours.

materials

Fabric: 2¼ yards 45"-wide green for skirt and backing, 7 (7" x 8") pieces in assorted prints for birdhouses, assorted scraps for roofs, posts, and other appliqués

1¼ yards string

Fabric marking pencil

Pushpin

42" square cotton batting

2½ yards tear-away stabilizer

Straight pins

2 yards Pellon® Wonder-Under®

Thread: black, variegated bright colored, green to match tree skirt, white, colors to match appliqués

4¼ yards white pom-pom trim

Finished Size: Approximately 40" in diameter

Instructions

Note: Seam allowances are ½".

1. For skirt and skirt backing circles, cut two 42" squares from green fabric. Fold each square in half from top to bottom, then fold in half again from left to right. Tie one end of string to point end of fabric marking pencil. Insert pushpin through string 20½" from attached pencil. Insert pushpin into folded corner of one fabric

square. Referring to Diagram, hold string taut and mark arc on fabric. Repeat to mark remaining square. To mark center opening in skirt, remove pushpin from fabric and string; reinsert pushpin into string 1¾" from pencil. Mark arc on one square as before. Repeat to mark remaining square. Cut along drawn arc lines, through all layers. Unfold circles. Using one circle as pattern,

cut one 41"-diameter circle from batting.

2. Fold one fabric circle in half three times. Press folds lightly. To make back opening, unfold circle and cut along one fold line from outer edge to inner circle. Pin stabilizer to wrong side of circle, cutting and piecing as necessary to fit. Baste stabilizer to skirt.

3. Referring to Appliqué-tions on page 10, press Wonder-Under onto wrong side of 7" x 8" fabric pieces and fabric scraps. Referring to photos, trace one Birdhouse A, two Birdhouse Bs (one with perch bar), two Birdhouse Cs, one Birdhouse D, one Birdhouse E, eight Trees, five Flying Birds, three Walking Birds, one Santa Cap, and one Bag onto Wonder-Under side of fabrics. For packages, draw

assorted squares and rectangles on Wonder-Under side of fabric. Cut out shapes along pattern lines. Remove paper backing.

4. Referring to photo, position one birdhouse post on right side of stabilized circle on each fold line, aligning one short end of post with outer edge of circle. Fuse posts in place. Position corresponding birdhouses on top of posts, and fuse in place in order indicated on pattern. In following order, fuse birds, trees, Santa cap (in order indicated), bag, and packages.

5. Using thread to match appliqués, satin-stitch around each piece. Referring to photos and patterns, use black thread to satin-stitch eyes on flying birds and eyes and legs on walking birds. Satin-stitch ribbons and bows on packages, loose string on bag, and cross on top of church. Using decorative machine stitches and variegated thread, stitch garlands on trees and birdhouses as desired. Remove basting and stabilizer.

6. For skirt back opening, cut undecorated fabric circle and batting circle from outer edge to inner circle. To assemble tree skirt, with edges and back openings aligned, layer batting, tree skirt front (right side up), and tree skirt back (right side down). Baste in place. Stitch skirt, batting, and backing together, leaving 9" opening along one straight edge of skirt. Trim excess batting, clip curves, and turn right side out. Slipstitch opening closed.

7. To machine-quilt tree skirt, using thread to match skirt, straight-stitch around appliquéd pieces and along marked fold lines, stitching through all thicknesses.

Diagram

Birdhouse A

Birdhouse B

Birdhouse B (with extension)

Birdhouse C

Birdhouse C

Birdhouse D

Birdhouse E

other ideas

Use the flying bird pattern to make tree ornaments to accompany your tree skirt.

8. To finish skirt, pin pom-pom trim to outer edges, leaving ¼" tail of trim on each end for turning under. Repeat to pin pom-pom trim to inner circle. Stitch close to edges of trim. Fold trim ends under and stitch.

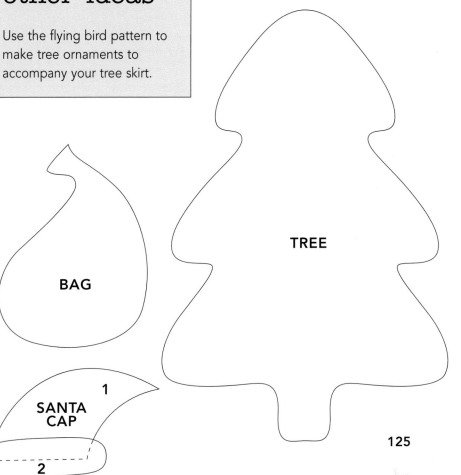

BAG

TREE

1

SANTA
CAP

2

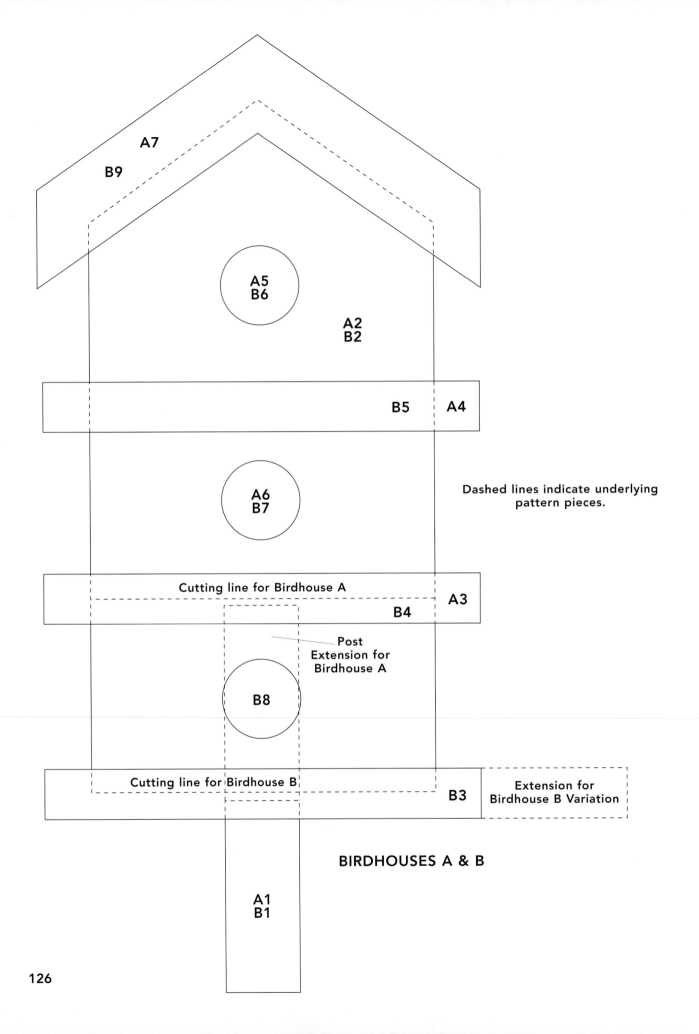

A7
B9

A5
B6

A2
B2

B5   A4

A6
B7

Cutting line for Birdhouse A

A3

B4

Dashed lines indicate underlying
pattern pieces.

Post
Extension for
Birdhouse A

B8

Cutting line for Birdhouse B

B3

Extension for
Birdhouse B Variation

BIRDHOUSES A & B

A1
B1

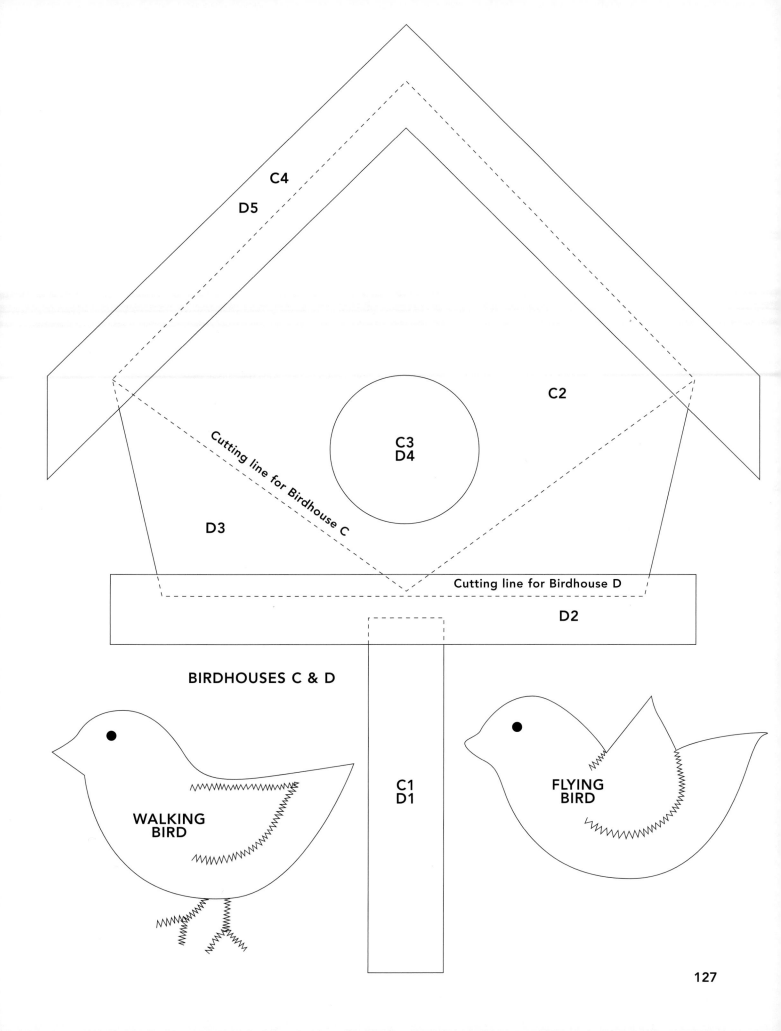

C4
D5

C2

C3
D4

Cutting line for Birdhouse C

D3

Cutting line for Birdhouse D

D2

BIRDHOUSES C & D

WALKING
BIRD

C1
D1

FLYING
BIRD

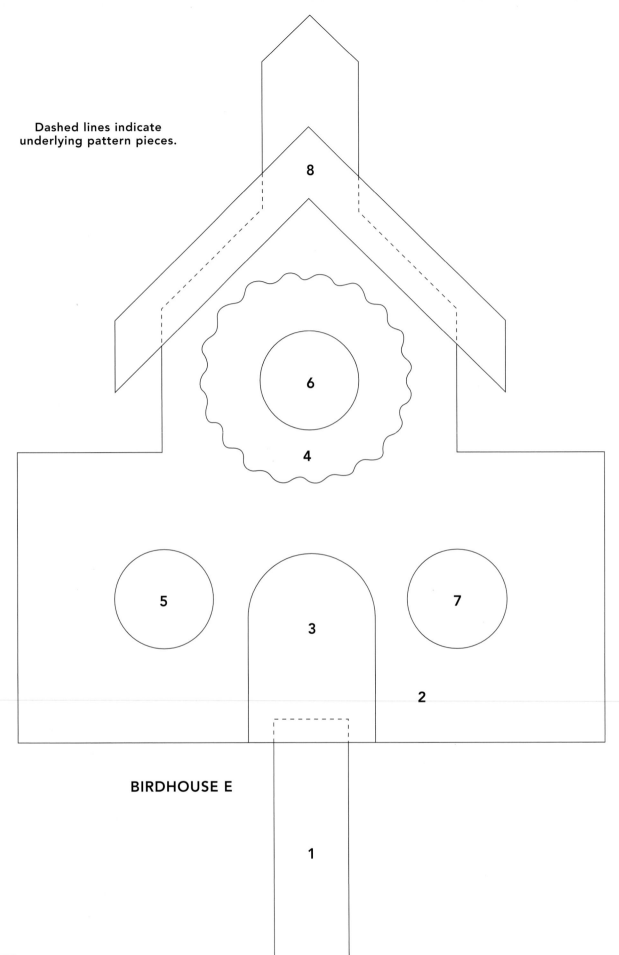

Dashed lines indicate
underlying pattern pieces.

8

6

4

5

3

7

2

BIRDHOUSE E

1

Pet Stockings

Include your pets in the holiday festivities by making them their own
personalized stockings. No sewing required.

materials

For each

½ yard Pellon® Heavy Duty Wonder-Under®

Embroidery needle

For Bone

Wool or felt: 3" square lime green; 1" x 3" piece each fuchsia, orange, light pink; 1" x 2" yellow piece; 12" x 10" purple piece

Yellow yarn

14" length ¼"-wide yellow ribbon

2 (⅜") pink heart buttons

Pink puffy fabric paint

For Mouse

Wool or felt: 3" x 4" pink piece, 4" x 8" orange piece, 8" x 12" red piece

1 (¼") black button

Straight pins

Pink pearl cotton

Ribbon: ½ yard ⅜"-wide red grosgrain, ⅓ yard ⅛"-wide red satin

Pink puffy fabric paint

For Fish

Wool or felt: 6" square each lime green, turquoise; 6" x 7" green piece; 2" square pink; 9" x 14" blue piece

Pony beads: 3 green, 5 pink, 3 blue, 3 red, 1 black

Straight pins

Pink pearl cotton

Lime green puffy fabric paint

Finished sizes: Bone, 10½" x 5¼"; Mouse, 7¼" x 5⅝"; Fish, 8⅜" x 6½"

Instructions for Bone Stocking

1. Trace shapes B, C, D, E, F, and G onto paper side of Wonder-Under. Leaving approximately ¼" margin, cut around shapes. Referring to Appliqué-tions on page 10 and to photo for colors, press Wonder-Under shapes onto wrong side of wool pieces. Cut out fabric shapes along pattern lines. Remove paper backings.

2. With wrong sides facing, fold purple wool piece in half width-wise. Trace outline of bone (shape A) onto purple wool. Cut out bone

along pattern lines. Referring to photo, fuse appliqué shapes in place on right side of one purple bone shape.

3. With wrong sides facing, stack purple bone shapes. Using yarn and stitching through all layers, make running stitches along edges of bone, leaving top edge open.

4. Cut 2 (3") lengths from ribbon. Fold each length in half. Tack one folded ribbon to appliquéd front of bone at each X. For hanger, slip one cut end of remaining ribbon piece between layers of bone at each X. Tack ribbon ends in place. Sew one heart button in place on top of each folded ribbon. Using fabric paint, write pet's name across top of bone.

Instructions for Mouse Stocking

1. Trace shapes B, C, D, E, F, and G onto paper side of Wonder-Under. Leaving approximately ¼" margin, cut around Wonder-Under shapes. Referring to Appliqué-tions on page 10, press shapes B and D onto wrong side of pink wool. Press remaining Wonder-Under shapes onto wrong side of orange wool. Cut out shapes along pattern lines. Remove paper backings from shapes B and D only. Referring to photo, center shape B on right side of shape C; center shape D on right side of shape E. Fuse shapes B and D in place. Remove paper backings from remaining appliqué pieces.

2. With wrong sides facing, fold red wool piece in half widthwise. Trace outline of mouse (shape A; including outline of shape E, but not shapes H) onto red wool. Trace shapes H onto right side of pink wool. Cut out shapes along pattern lines. Referring to photo, fuse shapes C, D, F, and G onto right side of one red mouse shape. Sew button in place for eye.

3. With wrong sides facing, stack red mouse shapes. Slip shapes H between layers of mouse where indicated on pattern. Pin shapes in place. Using one strand of pearl cotton and stitching through all layers, make running stitches along edges of mouse, leaving open between X 2 and X 3 on pattern. Remove pins.

4. For mouse tail and hanger, tie knot in one end of red grosgrain ribbon 2" from cut end. Tack unknotted end of ribbon to mouse, at X 1, stitching through all layers. Move up 4" on ribbon and tack at X 2; tack knot at opposite end of ribbon at X 3.

5. For whiskers, cut satin ribbon into three equal lengths. Holding lengths as one, tie knot in center of ribbon lengths. Tack knotted whiskers to nose of mouse. Using fabric paint, write pet's name across top of mouse.

Instructions for Fish Stocking

1. Trace shapes B, C, D, E, F, G, H, I, and J onto paper side of Wonder-Under. Leaving approximately ¼" margin, cut around shapes. Referring to Appliqué tions on page 10 and photo for colors, press Wonder-Under

shapes onto wrong side of wool pieces. Cut out shapes along pattern lines. Remove paper backing from shapes C, D, J, I, and H.

2. Referring to photo and pattern for placement, fuse shapes C and D to right side of shape B. Fuse shape J to right side of shape E. Remove paper backing from shape E; fuse shape E to right side of shape B. Fuse shapes I to right side of shape F. Remove paper backing from shape F; fuse shape F to right side of shape B. Fuse shape H to right side of shape G.

3. With wrong sides facing, fold blue wool piece in half widthwise. Trace outline of stocking (shape A) onto blue wool. Cut out stocking along pattern lines. Trace shapes K onto right side of pink wool. Cut

out shapes along pattern lines. Referring to photo, fuse appliquéd shapes G and B in place on right side of one blue stocking shape. Referring to photo for colors and placement, sew pony beads on stocking.

4. With wrong sides facing, stack blue stocking shapes. Slip shapes K between layers of stocking where indicated on pattern; pin shapes in place. Using one strand of pearl cotton and stitching through all layers, make running stitches along edges of stocking, leaving top open.

5. For hanger, fold ribbon in half and knot center. Tack knot to back of stocking at X. Using fabric paint, write pet's name across center of stocking.

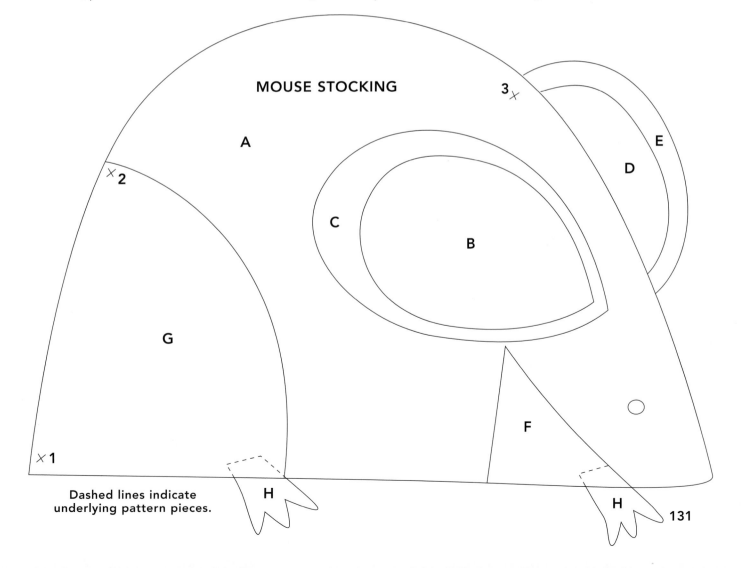

MOUSE STOCKING

Dashed lines indicate underlying pattern pieces.

131

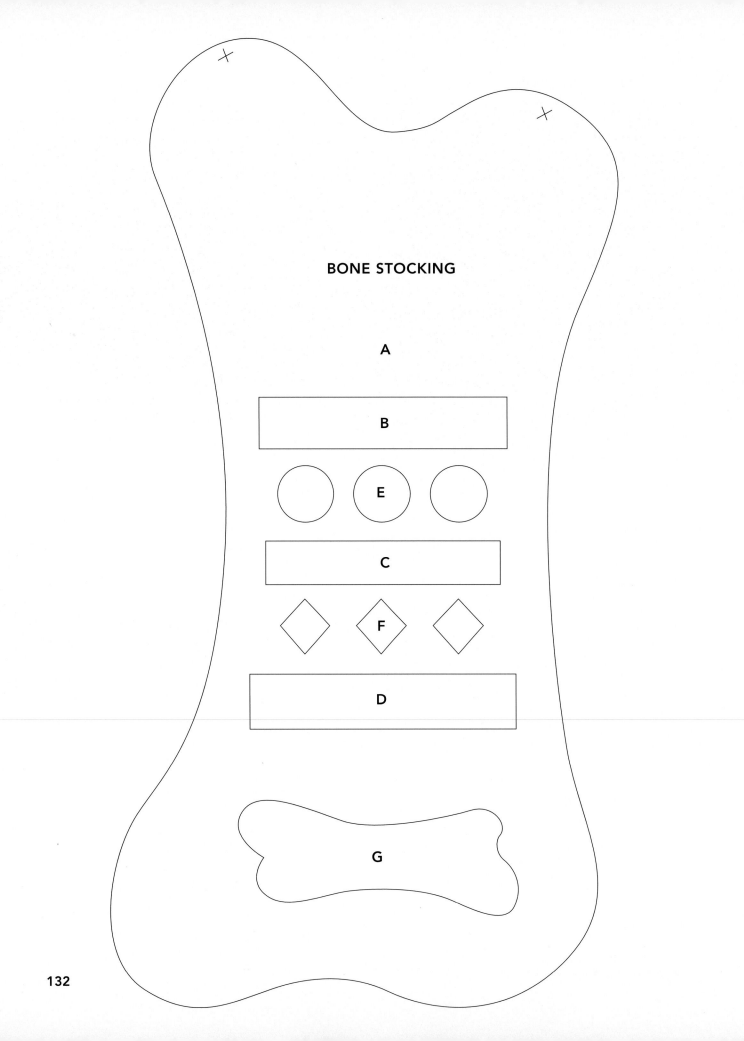

BONE STOCKING

A

B

E

C

F

D

G

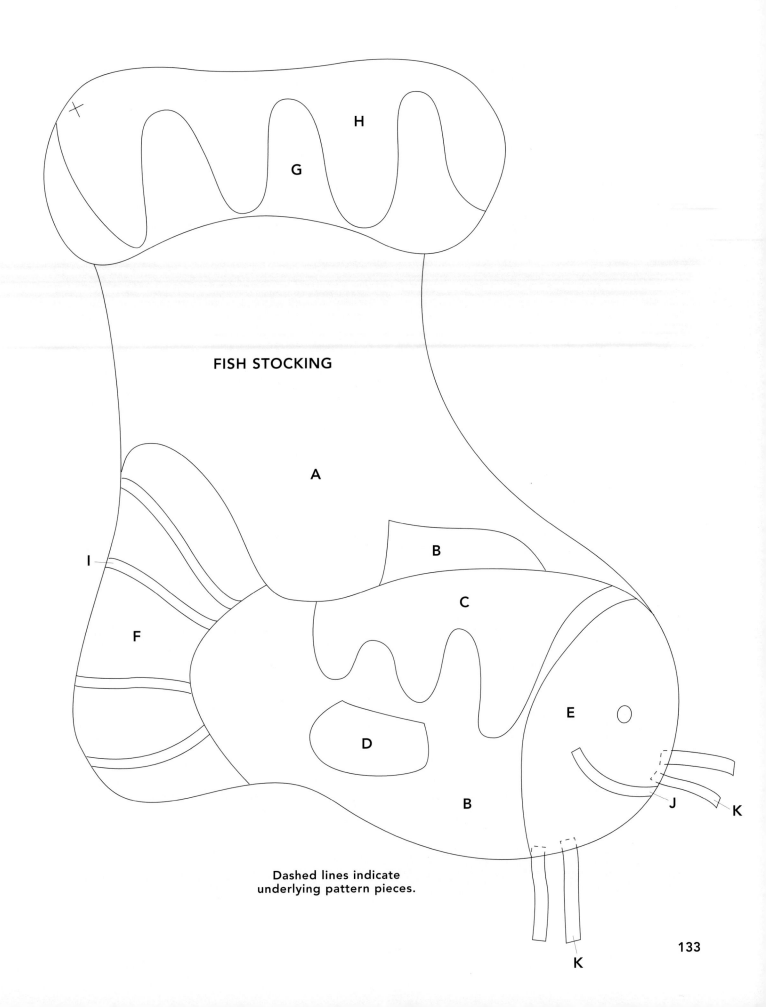

FISH STOCKING

Dashed lines indicate
underlying pattern pieces.

133

⊕rnament 𝒯ablecloth

Designed by Cynthia Moody Wheeler

our table for the holidays with this festive tablecloth. The garland of ornaments is cut
merry madras dish towels. You can cut as many as 12 ornament appliqués from one
. To complete your seasonal linen set, buy extra towels to use as oversized napkins.

naterials

sed 72" x 110" red-
hite striped tablecloth

d 20" x 28" plaid or
rd tea towels or dish

aring-ink fabric marker

s green jumbo
ck

green, colors to
towels, black

Pellon® Wonder-Under®

tear-away stabilizer

ize: 72" x 100"

ions

ing tablecloth other than
adjust amount of rick-
der-Under, and stabilizer
y.
ry, and iron tablecloth
, following manufactur-
tions. Place tablecloth
Jsing fabric marker, mar
where it drops off edge

g to photo, pin rickrack
th along marked lines,
ing it around corners.
k, leaving ½" excess on
or turning under. Stitch
er of rickrack.
ament appliqués, trace
pattern onto paper side

of Wonder-Under 36 times. (You
may apply fewer or more ornaments on your tablecloth.) Leaving
approximately ½" margin, cut
around shapes.

4. Referring to Appliqué-tions on
page 10, press Wonder-Under
shapes onto wrong sides of dish
towels. Cut out ornaments along
pattern lines and remove paper
backings.

5. Referring to photo, on right side
of tablecloth, randomly place ornament shapes approximately 1½"
below rickrack border. Place some

ornaments at an angle and cluster
or overlap others. Fuse ornaments
to tablecloth.

6. Cut stabilizer into 36 (6")
squares. On wrong side of tablecloth, center one stabilizer square
under each ornament. Using
medium satin stitch, stitch around
each ornament. For ornament cap,
using wide satin stitch, stitch two
rows. Referring to photo, use fabric marker to draw hook from each
ornament cap to rickrack. Using
narrow satin stitch, stitch along
marked hooks. Remove stabilizer.

de greeting cards.
use it doesn't bubbl
be smooth and neat

materials

For each card

Pellon® Wonder-Under® scraps

Assorted fabric scraps for appliqués

Plain purchased 5" x 7" note cards (or folded card stock) with matching envelopes

Black fine-tip permanent marker

For Girl

Embroidery needle

Ecru pearl cotton

1 (⅞") natural wood round button

Pink permanent marker

For Reindeer

Red permanent marker

For Snowman

Cotton batting scraps

Embroidery needle

For Santa

Cotton batting scraps

2 (⅜") black round buttons

Pink permanent marker

Embroidery needle

Finished size: 5" x 7"

Instructions for Girl Note Card and Envelope

Note: Use a dry press cloth for this project.

1. Referring to Appliqué-tions on page 10, press Wonder-Under onto wrong side of fabric scraps. Do not remove paper backing. Trace two hats, two hatbands, two faces, one scarf, and one body onto Wonder-Under side of fabric scraps. Cut out fabric shapes along pattern lines. Remove paper backings.

2. Referring to photo and pattern, fuse one of each girl piece to center front of card in order indicated. Fuse one hat, hatband, and face to lower left corner of envelope front in order indicated.

3. To embellish, thread embroidery needle with pearl cotton; do not knot. Position button on scarf. Working from top of button, push needle down through one hole and through top layer of card. Push needle back up through opposite hole. Tie pearl cotton in knot on top of button; trim ends. For scarf fringe, stitch and tie knots, in same manner, along ends of scarf.

4. To finish card and envelope, using black marker, draw pen stitching around outline of girl; draw hair and eyes. Using pink marker, draw and smudge cheeks on girl's face.

Instructions for Reindeer Note Card and Envelope

Note: Use a dry press cloth for this project.

1. Referring Appliqué-tions on page 10, press Wonder-Under onto wrong side of fabric scraps. Referring to Step 1 for Girl, trace one reindeer, one ornament, nine holly leaves, and six holly berries. Referring to photo and pattern, fuse reindeer, ornament, six holly leaves, and three holly berries to center front of note card in order indicated. Fuse three holly leaves and three holly berries to lower left corner of envelope front.

2. To finish card and envelope, using black marker, draw pen stitching along edges of reindeer; draw eyes and mouth. Using red marker, draw nose.

Instructions for Snowman Note Card and Envelope

Note: Use a dry press cloth for this project.

1. Referring to Appliqué-tions on page 10, press Wonder-Under onto wrong side of fabric scraps. Referring to Step 1 for Girl and photo, trace one full snowman, one snowman from chest up, one scarf, one pair of twig arms, two hats, two hatbands, and two noses. Referring to photo and pattern, fuse full snowman, twig arms, scarf, one hat, one hatband, and one nose to center front of note card in order indicated. Fuse snowman from chest up, one hat, one hatband, and one nose to lower left corner of envelope front.

2. Press Wonder-Under onto one side of cotton batting. Do not remove paper backing. Trace two pom-poms onto Wonder-Under side of batting. Cut out shapes along pattern lines. Remove paper backings. To embellish, fuse one pom-pom to end of hat on note card; fuse remaining pom-pom to end of hat on envelope. Referring to Step 3 for Girl, stitch and tie knots along ends of scarf.

3. To finish card and envelope, using black marker, draw pen stitching along edges of snowman and nose; draw eyes.

Instructions for Santa Note Card and Envelope

Note: Use a dry press cloth for this project.

1. Referring to Appliqué-tions on page 10, press Wonder-Under onto wrong side of fabric scraps and onto one side of cotton batting. Do not remove paper backing. Referring to Step 1 for Girl, trace Santa pieces and package pieces. (Pom-pom on top of hat, trim around bottom of hat, beard, cuffs on sleeves, and trim around bottom of coat are cut from batting.) Referring to photo and pattern, fuse Santa pieces to center front of note card in order indicated. Fuse package pieces to lower left corner of envelope front in order indicated.

2. To embellish, referring to Step 3 for Girl, attach black round buttons to center front of Santa.

3. To finish card and envelope, using black marker, draw pen stitching along edges of Santa's coat; draw eyes. Using pink marker, draw and smudge cheeks on Santa's face.

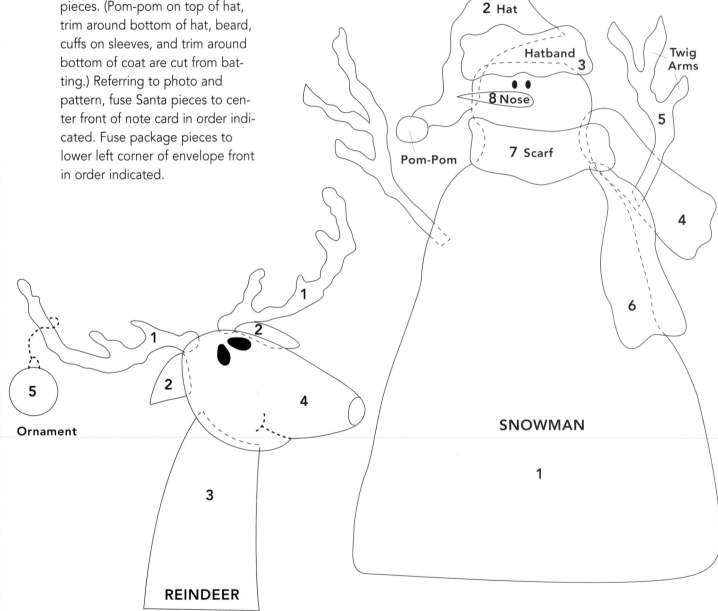

Light dashes indicate lines of underlying pattern pieces.
Bold dashes indicate drawn lines.

138

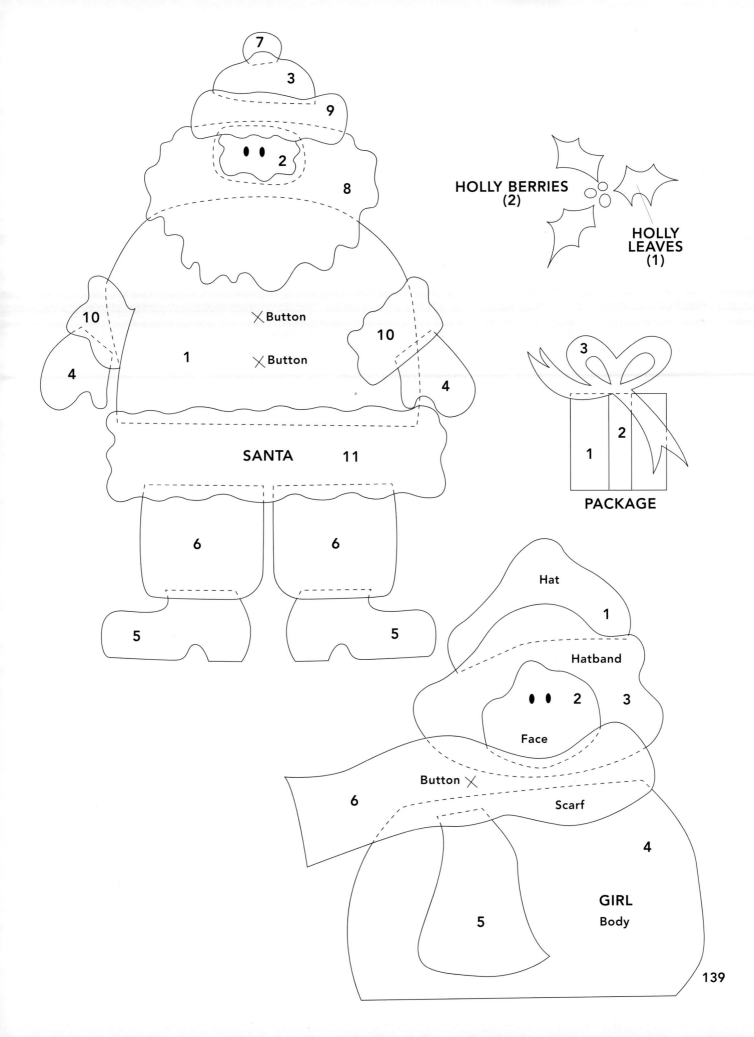

HOLLY BERRIES
(2)

HOLLY
LEAVES
(1)

PACKAGE

3

2

1

7

3

9

2

8

10

Button

Button

1

10

4

4

SANTA 11

6

6

5

5

Hat

1

Hatband

2

3

Face

Button

6

Scarf

4

5

GIRL
Body

139

page 158

page 147

page 144

Gift-Giving Wonders

Handmade presents are always the most treasured gifts. Show how much you care by giving some of the fun-to-make items found in this chapter. Many of the projects are so quick, you can easily finish them in time for those last-minute gift-giving occasions.

Pearls-of-Wisdom Pincushion

Designed by Linda Hendrickson

Make it a point to give this handy pincushion to a friend who sews. She's bound
to appreciate the wise words written along the edges.

materials

Pellon® Wonder-Under® scraps

Fabric: burgundy-and-black
  checked scraps, ⅛ yard
  burgundy cotton, ¼ yard
  black cotton

Burgundy thread

White fine-tip permanent
  fabric marker

Beading needle

Glass beads: burgundy, black

Burgundy bugle beads

4 (¼") black shank buttons

Stuffing

Finished Size: 5½" x 6"

Instructions

1. Trace heart onto paper side of Wonder-Under twice. Draw four ½" squares, two ½" x 2½" rectangles, two ½" x 3" rectangles, and two ¼" x 2¾" rectangles onto paper side of Wonder-Under. Leaving approximately ¼" margin, cut around shapes.

2. Referring to Appliqué-tions on page 10, press ¼" x 2¾" Wonder-Under rectangles onto wrong side of burgundy-and-black checked fabric on bias. Press remaining Wonder-Under shapes onto wrong side of burgundy fabric. Cut out shapes along pattern lines. Remove paper backings from burgundy-and-black checked rectangles only.

3. Center and stack one checked rectangle, faceup, on right side of each ½" x 3" burgundy rectangle. Fuse checked rectangles in place.

4. From black fabric, cut two 6" x 6½" pieces for pincushion front and back. To mark center, fold front piece in half from right to left and then in half again from top to bottom. Referring to Diagram, use creases as guide to position appliqué pieces on pincushion front. Fuse appliqués in place. Using narrow satin stitch and burgundy thread, stitch around edges of each appliqué.

5. Using white pen, print "A PIN IN THE CUSHION" across top edge of pincushion front. Turn pincushion front so that tips of hearts are at top, and print "IS WORTH TWO IN THE CHAIR" across edge.

6. With right sides facing and raw edges aligned, fold pincushion top in half so that hearts are facing; press. Referring to photograph and using center crease as a guide,

stitch bugle beads and burgundy glass beads in place with beading needle. Stitch bugle beads along each side rectangle. Stitch black glass beads between each bugle bead. Stitch one button in center of each burgundy square.

8. With right sides facing and raw edges aligned, stitch pincushion front to back, using ¼" seam and leaving 2" opening. Turn right side out and stuff firmly. Slipstitch opening closed.

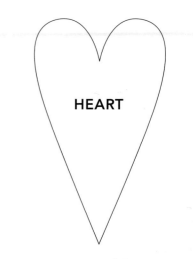

HEART

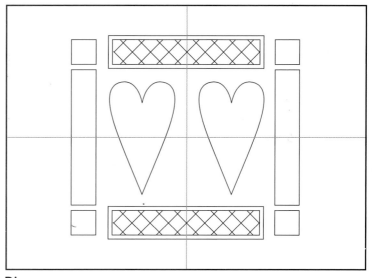

Diagram
Gray crossed lines indicate creases.

Veggie Kitchen Towels

Adorn ordinary kitchen towels with these fresh-picked appliqués.
The outlines of the produce become the corner of the towel!

materials

3 woven cotton kitchen towels

Fabric (⅛ yard each): red calico; green, red, yellow, lavender, purple, and tan solid; white muslin

½ yard Pellon® Wonder-Under®

Dressmaker's carbon

Thread: red, green, yellow, lavender, purple, tan

Water-soluble stabilizer

Instructions

1. Wash and dry towels and fabrics. Do not use fabric softener in washer or dryer. Referring to Appliqué-tions on page 10, press Wonder-Under onto wrong side of appliqué fabrics (including white muslin).

2. Trace one tomato and one tomato slice edge onto Wonder-Under side of red calico. Trace one pepper, two eggplant stems, and one tomato stem to Wonder-Under side of green fabric. Trace one tomato slice to Wonder-Under side of red fabric. Reverse pattern and trace one pepper to Wonder-Under side of yellow fabric. Trace one eggplant each to Wonder-Under sides of lavender and purple fabrics. Trace one pepper stem to Wonder-Under side of tan fabric; reverse pattern and trace again. Cut out shapes along pattern lines. Using dressmaker's carbon and following manufacturer's instructions, transfer details to each appliqué. Remove paper backings.

3. Fuse appliqués to right side of muslin fabric, using dashed-line placement guide to assemble appliqués. Cut out each piece with muslin backing; remove paper backing from muslin.

4. Referring to photo and Diagram, fuse appliqué pieces to lower left-hand corner of towels. Using matching thread, satin-stitch internal details on appliqués. Trim excess towel fabric from corner, following outline of appliqués. Referring to manufacturer's instructions, apply water-soluble stabilizer around outside edges of appliqués; satin-stitch edges. Remove stabilizer.

other ideas

Use these same veggie motifs to decorate your windows. For a harvest-fresh valance, join kitchen towels along short ends until valance is desired width. For casing, fold one long edge 2" to back and stitch. Apply veggie appliqués to front of valance along hem.

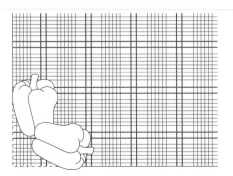

Diagram
Dashed line indicates corner of towel to trim.

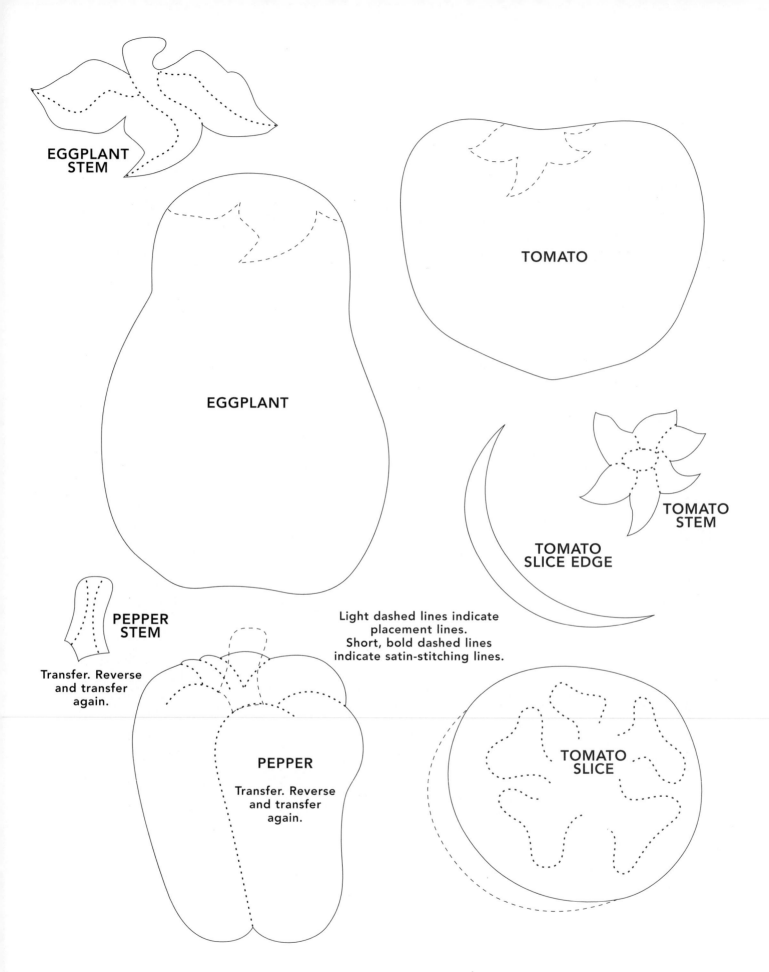

EGGPLANT
STEM

TOMATO

EGGPLANT

TOMATO
STEM

TOMATO
SLICE EDGE

PEPPER
STEM

Transfer. Reverse
and transfer
again.

Light dashed lines indicate
placement lines.
Short, bold dashed lines
indicate satin-stitching lines.

PEPPER

Transfer. Reverse
and transfer
again.

TOMATO
SLICE

Stolen Hearts Pillow

Show your sweetie that you love him just as much today as when he
first stole your heart—present him with this handsome throw pillow. It's a great way
to give new life to outdated neckties.

materials

1⅝ yards ⅜"-wide grosgrain ribbon

14" square osnaburg fabric (or other coarse cotton cloth) for pillow front

Fabric glue

Disappearing-ink fabric marker

10 neckties*

Seam ripper

Pellon® Wonder-Under® scraps

Coordinating color embroidery floss

Embroidery needle

14" square fabric for pillow back

Thread to match fabrics

1⅝ yards ⅜"-diameter cotton cord

Zipper foot attachment

Stuffing

*You can find inexpensive neckties at thrift stores.

Finished Size: Approximately 13" square

Instructions

1. Cut four 14" lengths from ribbon. Referring to photo and Diagram, position ribbon lengths on pillow front. Glue ribbons in place. Using disappearing-ink fabric marker, mark ½" seam allowance along edges of pillow front.

2. For each tie, use seam ripper to carefully open tie along center back seam; trim away lining and press tie flat. Cut one 4" square from eight different ties. From Wonder-Under, cut eight 3¾" squares. Referring to Appliqué-tions on page 10, press one Wonder-Under square onto wrong side of each tie square. Do not remove paper backings. Trace one heart pattern onto Wonder-Under side of each square. Cut out hearts along pattern lines. Remove paper backings.

3. Referring to Diagram, center hearts in ribbon squares and fuse in place. Referring to Diagram A on page 56 and using three strands of embroidery floss, blanket-stitch around each heart. Using disappearing-ink fabric marker, write "You stole my heart" in remaining square. Referring to Diagram C on page 56 and using two strands of embroidery floss, outline-stitch words.

4. From remaining ties, cut one 1½" x 56" strip, piecing as necessary. To make cording, lay cord along center of wrong side of tie strip. Fold strip over cord, matching long edges. Using zipper foot attachment, machine-baste along length of strip close to cord. Matching raw edges and beginning 1" from end of cording, baste cording to right side of pillow front, clipping seam allowances as necessary. Open ends of cording and cut cord to fit exactly. Insert one end of tie fabric into other; fold raw edge of top tie fabric ½" to wrong side and baste in place.

5. With right sides facing, raw edges aligned, and using zipper foot attachment, stitch pillow front to pillow back, stitching close to cording and leaving opening for turning.

6. Turn pillow right side out and press. Stuff pillow. Slipstitch opening closed.

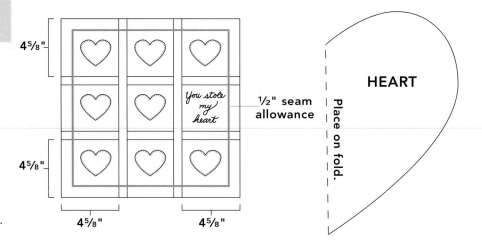

Diagram

4⅝"

4⅝"

4⅝"

4⅝"

½" seam allowance

HEART

Place on fold.

Welcome Banner

Nothing makes you feel more at home than a warm country welcome. This no-sew project is great fun to make because perfection is not the objective. Part of the banner's down-home charm comes from its skewed lines and uneven edges.

materials

¼ yard muslin

8" x 31" piece blue print fabric for sky, backing, and various appliqués

1 yard Pellon® Wonder-Under®

8" x 20" piece golden brown print fabric for house

Assorted plaid and miniprint fabric scraps for remaining appliqués

Rotary cutter, mat, and quilter's ruler

Burgundy embroidery floss

Embroidery needle

24 assorted round buttons

1 small black bead for bird's eye

Dressmaker's carbon

Black permanent marker

Finished Size: 7½" x 22½"

Instructions

1. Cut 8" x 23" piece of muslin for banner foundation.

Designed by Linda Hendrickson

2. From blue print fabric and from Wonder-Under, cut one 8" x 5½" piece for sky and one 8" x 23" piece for backing. From golden brown fabric and Wonder-Under, cut one 8" x 14" piece for house. From plaid scrap and Wonder-Under, cut one 8" x 3½" piece for ground. Referring to Appliqué-tions on page 10, press Wonder-Under pieces onto wrong side of corresponding fabric pieces. Remove paper backings.

3. Fuse 8" x 23" blue backing piece to one side of muslin foundation. With top and side edges aligned, fuse 8" x 5½" blue sky piece to muslin side of foundation. With sides aligned, fuse 8" x 14" golden brown house piece to muslin foundation, but-ting top edge of golden brown piece against bottom edge of blue sky piece. With sides aligned, fuse 8" x 3½" plaid ground piece to muslin foundation, butting top edge of plaid piece against bot-tom edge of golden brown house piece. Using rotary cutter and quil-ter's ruler, trim ¼" off each side of banner.

4. Press Wonder-Under onto wrong side of remaining fabrics. Referring to photo and Diagram, and using patterns on page 151, roughly cut following appliqués: one chimney, one roof, one gutter, one cornice, two windows, two window ledges, one heart, one bird, one awning, one porch, one door, two large trees, one small tree, one threshold, one base of house, and one circle. Remove paper backings.

5. Referring to photo, fuse appli-qués in place. Using burgundy

150

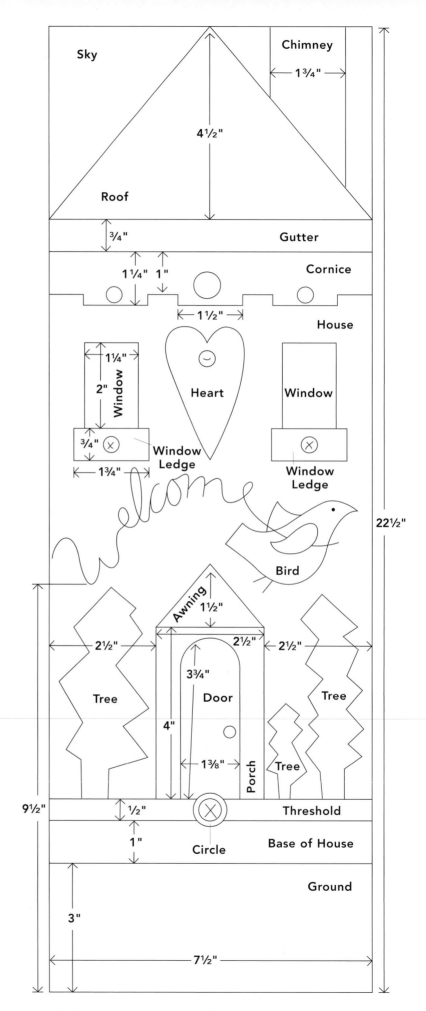

Diagram

embroidery floss and referring to photo, stitch buttons in place on cornice, heart, window ledges, door, and circle. Stitch bead in place for bird's eye. Using dressmaker's carbon, trace "Welcome" on banner where indicated on Diagram. Use black marker to mark over traced line. Draw bird's feet using black marker.

6. For hanger loops, thread needle with six strands of embroidery floss. Knot end of floss. For right hanger loop, working from back of banner, push needle through top edge of banner approximately ½" from side edge. Stitching through opposite holes, thread eight buttons onto floss. Push needle back through to back of banner. Tie off floss. Repeat to make left hanger loop.

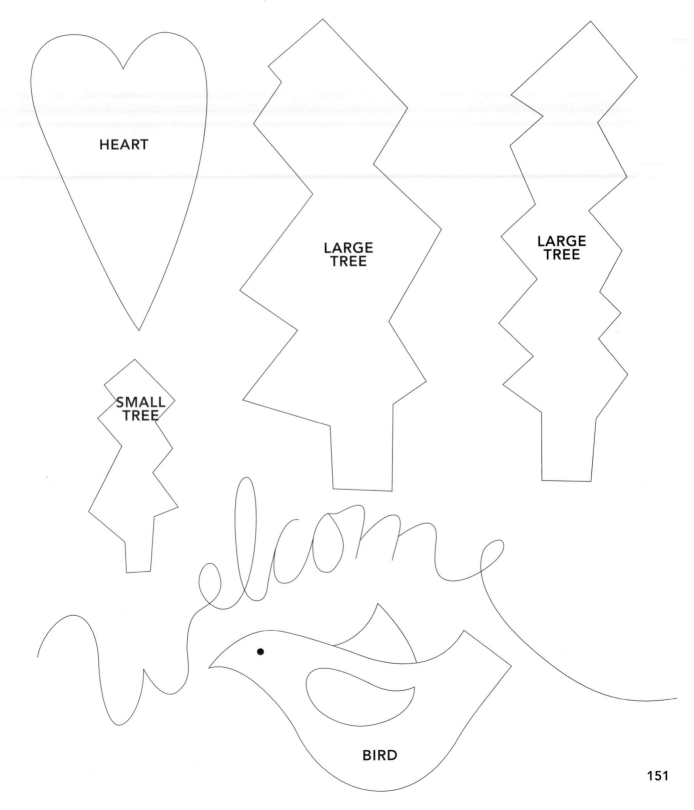

HEART

LARGE TREE

LARGE TREE

SMALL TREE

BIRD

Anniversary Album

Store precious family photos collected throughout your marriage in this elegant keepsake album. The folk art appliqués are easy to apply using fusible web.

materials

⅓ yard Pellon® Wonder-Under®

Ultrasuede®: 8" x 12" piece for birds, hearts, tulips, and base leaves; 5" square for flower petals, flower base, bird wings, curls at base of hearts, and ovals; 2"x 3½" piece for flower center and wings; 12¼" x 32" piece for background

Tracing paper

Thread to match Ultrasuede

14 seed beads

Coordinating pearl cotton

Embroidery needle

Rotary cutter

10½" x 11¾" x 2" photo album

Finished Size: 10½" x 11¾" x 2"

Instructions

1. Trace appliqué shapes onto paper side of Wonder-Under. Leaving approximately ¼" margin, cut around shapes. Referring to Appliqué-tions on page 10, press Wonder-Under shapes onto wrong side of corresponding Ultrasuede pieces. (*Note:* To preserve nap, use steam and lightly glide iron over shapes to bond layers.) Cut out Ultrasuede shapes along pattern lines. Remove paper backings.

2. To assist with placement, trace entire design onto tracing paper. Position background piece so that one long edge faces you. To position design horizontally, place traced design so that outermost tip of right-hand bird's tail is 5¾" from right-hand edge of background piece. Center design vertically. Using traced design as a guide, position appliqués on background piece. (Do not position flower center, flower base, or bird wings.) Using damp press cloth and lots of steam, fuse appliqués in place by lightly gliding iron over shapes. Position and fuse flower center and bird wings in place, in same manner. Fuse flower base in place.

3. Using matching thread, topstitch edges of birds, birds' wings, hearts, flower petals, flower base, and base leaves. Referring to photo, sew one seed bead in place on each bird for eye; sew three seed beads in place above each curl. Using pearl cotton and embroidery needle, and referring to photo and Diagram A, blanket-stitch lower edges of wings (not bird wings) and flower center. Referring to photo and Diagram B, make four lazy daisy stitches just above each oval to form flower. Referring to photo and Diagram C, make French knot in center of lazy daisy flowers.

4. To make album cover pockets, fold right-hand edge and left-hand edge of background piece 4" to wrong side. To secure pockets, stitch along long edges of background piece, ⅛" from edge. Use rotary cutter to trim edges if necessary.

5. To place cover on album, slip right-hand pocket over front cover of album. Gently fold album back and slip left-hand pocket over back cover.

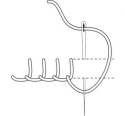

Diagram A - Blanket Stitch

Diagram B - Lazy Daisy Stitch

Diagram C - French Knot

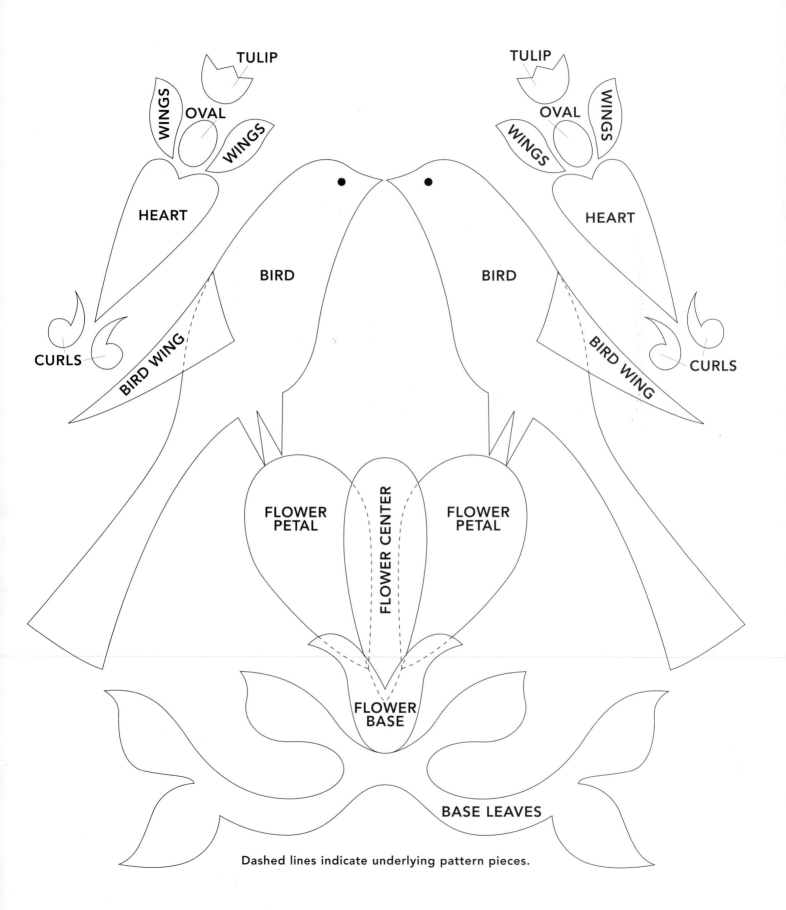

TULIP

WINGS

OVAL

WINGS

HEART

CURLS

BIRD

BIRD WING

BIRD

TULIP

OVAL

WINGS

WINGS

HEART

CURLS

BIRD WING

FLOWER PETAL

FLOWER CENTER

FLOWER PETAL

FLOWER BASE

BASE LEAVES

Dashed lines indicate underlying pattern pieces.

Checkbook Chic

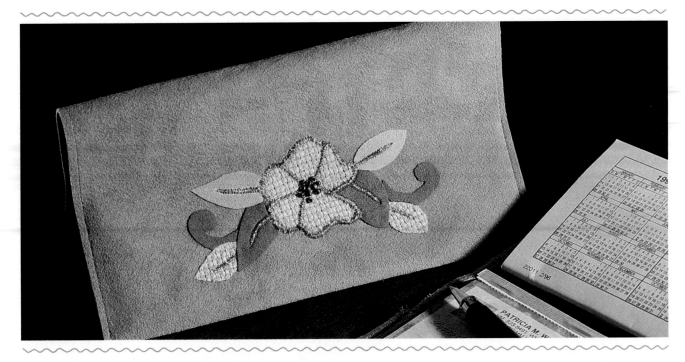

This sophisticated yet durable checkbook cover is a great way to make use of any Ultrasuede scraps left over from the album cover.

materials

Ultrasuede®: 7" x 11" piece for background, scraps for appliqués

Pellon® Wonder-Under® scraps

Fabric scraps

Metallic thread (optional)

Metallic fabric paint (optional)

11 seed beads

Needle and thread

Checkbook

Finished Size: Approximately 3⅝" x 6⅞"

1. Cut a 7" x 11" background piece from Ultrasuede. Referring to Step 1 of Anniversary Album, trace shapes onto scraps of Wonder-Under; press shapes onto wrong side of Ultrasuede scraps or fabric scraps. Position background piece so that one short edge faces you. Referring to Step 2 of Anniversary Album, center and fuse appliqués in place 3¾" above lower short edge of background piece.

2. Using metallic thread, satin-stitch veins on leaves and around petals of flower. Alternately, use metallic fabric paint in place of satinstitching. Sew 11 seed beads to center of flower.

3. To make pockets, fold each short edge of background piece 2" to wrong side. Refer to Step 4 of Anniversary Album to stitch and trim edges. Slip cover over front and back flaps of checkbook.

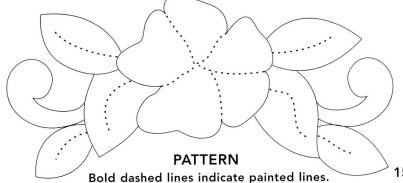

PATTERN
Bold dashed lines indicate painted lines.

155

Angelic Eyeglass Case

Designed by Cynthia Moody Wheeler

Let a guardian angel protect your eyeglasses! Or give a case to a
forgetful friend who tends to leave her glasses lying around. Quilters can use
this case for storing a rotary cutter.

materials

(For one eyeglass case)

⅛ yard Pellon® Wonder-Under®

Fabric: 3½" square gold or lamé for star, 3" x 4" piece gold or lamé for wings, 4" x 5½" piece white for angel body, 1½" square flesh color for head, 2 (4" x 15") pieces for case

Straight pins

4½" x 15½" piece tear-away stabilizer

Thread to match fabrics

4½" x 15½" piece batting

2 snaps

Finished Size: Approximately 3½" x 7"

Instructions

1. Trace angel body, head, wings, and star onto paper side of Wonder-Under. Leaving approximately ¼" margin, cut around shapes. Referring to Appliqué-tions on page 10, press Wonder-Under shapes onto wrong side of corresponding appliqué fabrics. Cut out shapes along pattern lines. Remove paper backings.

2. To form flap, with wrong sides facing, fold down 2¾" on one short end of eyeglass case fabric and lightly press fold. Center star horizontally on flap, positioning so that lower points of star are ⅜" from bottom raw edge of flap. Fuse star in place.

3. With wrong sides facing, fold remaining short end of eyeglass case up until case measures 7" in length. Lightly press fold. Tuck this raw end under flap. Center angel body on bottom section of case so that angel's arms are just touching bottom of star. Hold angel body in place by pinning bottom of skirt. Fold flap out of way and slip wings in place behind angel body. Remove pins from skirt and fuse wings and angel body in place. Position head over angel body and fuse in place.

4. Unfold case entirely and remove folds by pressing. Position tear-away stabilizer behind appliqués, and satin-stitch around each piece using medium-width satin stitch and matching thread. Remove excess stabilizer.

5. Center appliquéd piece on top of batting and pin pieces together. Zigzag-stitch around raw edges of appliquéd piece. Trim excess batting. With right sides facing and edges aligned, pin appliquéd piece and remaining 4" x 15" fabric piece together. Stitch edges using ¼" seam and leaving 2" opening along one long edge for turning. Trim corners and turn right side out. Fold raw edges of opening to inside. Press. Using matching thread and stitching close to edges, stitch around entire unfolded case, stitching opening closed in process.

6. Fold flap of case down 2½" and pin fold. Fold up bottom of case and position under flap, so that angel's arms touch bottom of star. Pin case along sides. Remove pins from flap and unfold flap so it is out of way. To make pocket of case, stitch bottom section along sides, using previous stitching as guide. Backstitch at beginning and end.

7. Sew half of each snap set in place on upper layer of pocket, positioning snaps just above each hand. Sew remaining half of each snap set to underside of flap, positioning snaps so that when flap is down, angel's hands will just touch bottom of star.

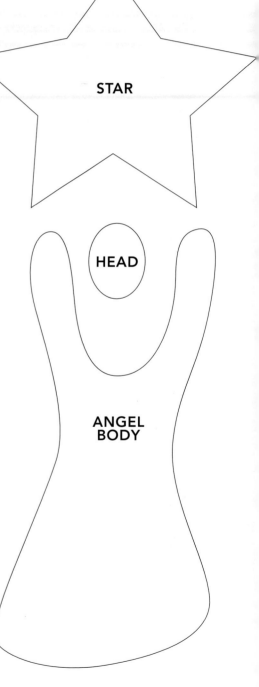

STAR

HEAD

ANGEL
BODY

158

Summertime Note Cards

These whimsical note cards are easy and fun to make. They're great for sending a quick letter or for inviting friends to a Fourth of July party or a watermelon cutting!

materials

For each

Pellon® Wonder-Under® scraps

Assorted fabric scraps for appliqués

Black fine-tip permanent marker

For Girl

Plain purchased 4" x 5¼" note card (or folded card stock) with matching envelope

Needle and thread

¼" round button

Pink permanent marker

For Flag

Plain purchased 5" x 7" note card (or folded card stock) with matching envelope

Finished Size for Girl Note Card: 4" x 5¼"

Finished Size for Flag Note Card: 5" x 7"

Instructions for Girl Note Card and Envelope

Note: Use a dry press cloth for this project.

1. Referring to Appliqué-tions on page 10, press Wonder-Under onto wrong side of fabric scraps. Trace one of each girl shape on page 160 onto Wonder-Under side of fabric scraps; trace two ladybugs. Cut out shapes along pattern lines. Remove paper backings.

2. Referring to photo and pattern, fuse one of each girl piece and one ladybug to center front of card in order indicated. Fuse remaining ladybug to lower left corner of envelope front.

3. To embellish card, thread needle and, referring to photo, sew button in place on hair bow. Using black marker, draw pen stitching around outline of girl head, hair bow, and top edge of watermelon slice; draw hair and eyes on girl; draw head, antennae, and legs on ladybugs. Using pink marker, draw and smudge cheeks on girl's face.

Instructions for Flag Note Card and Envelope

Note: Use a dry press cloth for this project.

1. Referring to Appliqué-tions on page 10, press Wonder-Under onto wrong side of fabric scraps. Trace one large star and one small star on page 160 onto Wonder-Under side of fabric scraps; draw three ½" x 3" strips, three ½" x 5½" strips, and one 1¾" x 2⅜" rectangle. Cut out shapes along pattern lines. Remove paper backings.

2. Referring to photo and pattern, fuse strips and rectangle to center front of note card. Fuse large star in place on top of rectangle. Fuse small star to lower left corner of envelope front.

3. To finish card and envelope, using black marker, draw pen stitching around outside of stripes and rectangle; draw pen stitching along edges of large star and around outside of small star.

hottip
double the pleasure

For an extra-sturdy project, use Heavy Duty Wonder-Under. Or fuse two layers of fabric together using Heavy Duty Wonder-Under. You'll get a stiff, heavy, reversible fabric that you can use to make Christmas ornaments and jewelry.

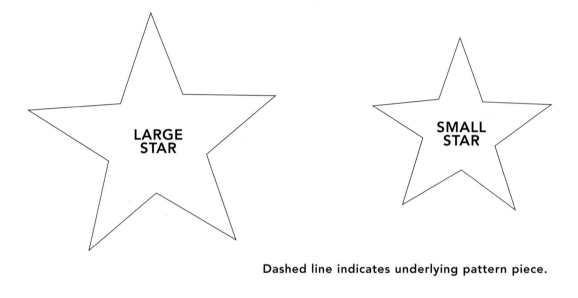

LARGE STAR

SMALL STAR

Dashed line indicates underlying pattern piece.

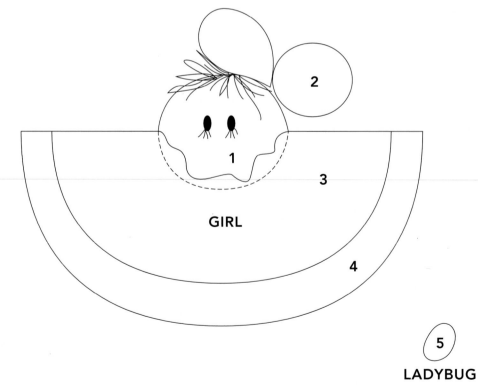

2

1

3

GIRL

4

5

LADYBUG